1. *A Japanese-style arrangement, utilising a gorse branch, Carlton daffodils and a bract of long-lasting evergreen senecio rotundofolia. Stems are held on pinholder in a small container hidden beneath the moss. An arrangement that will last a long time with just a 'face lift' of fresh flowers*

Joyce Rogers

FLOWER ARRANGING

Hamlyn

London · New York · Sydney · Toronto

TO LESLIE — MY HUSBAND AND HELPMATE

Contents

Published by
THE HAMLYN PUBLISHING GROUP LIMITED
LONDON · NEW YORK · SYDNEY · TORONTO
Astronaut House, Feltham, Middlesex, England

First published in 1964
Twelfth impression 1975
© The Hamlyn Publishing Group Limited, 1964
ISBN 0 600 33479 1

Printed in Hong Kong by Toppan Printing Co. Ltd.

Introduction

Practically everyone appreciates beauty, although different people may have very different ideas as to the kind of beauty which gives them the most pleasure. For example, some will be happiest with a very formal design in their garden, others will prefer a more natural layout which echoes the wildness of the countryside. By the same token, you may like your flowers in a formally executed mass design, whereas your neighbour may prefer fewer flowers, very simply arranged. These are individual choices, reflecting different tastes and personalities, but they are all related to a basic appreciation of art, to that dormant artistic streak which exists in everyone. Once brought to life it can never be satisfied until you actually experience the joy of creating beauty for yourself.

This, I think, is why so many people turn to one or other of the art forms for self expression. Of these, flower arranging is one of the arts that can be learned and practised most easily, which probably explains its continuous growth in popularity. Its direct relationship to horticulture, to the never failing magic of growing things, is perhaps another reason for its increasing following. Nevertheless there are many people who appreciate the beauty of good flower arrangement, but have absolutely no idea how they should go about it.

It was with the purpose of showing you how that I wrote this book. I also hope it will meet the many requests from past and present pupils who have so often asked me 'to set down in print what you so helpfully explain in class'. So here is the final result, although I must admit it would be much easier for me to pick up flowers and foliage, and to show you what to do, rather than try to put it into words.

Nevertheless, I have tried to really help beginners by explaining the basic principles and techniques of flower arranging. I think the more experienced will also benefit by my look-and-learn course of instruction, particularly with regard to the more complicated all-round dinner table arrangements, for which I have formulated a genuinely easy method. I have also included a special chapter on the understanding and use of colour, a subject which is not only of great importance but of great interest.

I would like to express my very great appreciation to the Flowers and Plants Council, for whom I was privileged to create most of the illustrated arrangements. I would also like to say thank you to my two photographers, Ronald Sleep of Torquay and Roy Rich of P.R. Visuals, London, with whom I have worked in complete harmony while creating the arrangements in this book. And finally, to my artist Dorothy Fitchew for her excellent line sketches, miraculously created from my very rough preliminary drawings.

I COMPOSITION – BASIC PRINCIPLES

Express yourself — you cannot create by copying — follow the principles and evolve your own designs

Composing a beautiful picture is an art. And whether you choose stone, bricks or living materials, such as flowers and foliage, the art must be learned before your picture can be successful.

A lot has been written and said on this subject and some people are of the opinion that art is art and there are no rules. This simply is not true. In genuine art there must be rules, although once learned they can be *interpreted freely* to allow full expression of the artist's own personality and to give life to his creations.

In all the arts, composition is based upon universal natural principles, upon an understanding of forms and colours, variety and movement — in fact, upon the living elements of the universe itself. It is the student's task to learn to capture these abstracts so that all the various elements may be organised into one harmonious unit.

This chapter, with its discussion of art in general, and its comparison of flower arrangement with the other arts, will I hope, help to give you a clear understanding of the basic principles which govern all art forms. Once you have grasped these, you will be ready to learn the five basic rules of flower arrangement which are described · in Chapter II.

An autumn composition of fruit and vegetables in a striking line design. The branch of apple is held in position in water on an extra heavy pinholder with a large moulding of Plasticine built up behind it for extra support. The lowest cluster of three rosy apples, offset by the two colourful begonia leaves, mark the focal point, behind which all stems converge. The soft green grapes repeat the main colouring of these leaves and are texturally in harmony with them, both materials possessing a soft bloom

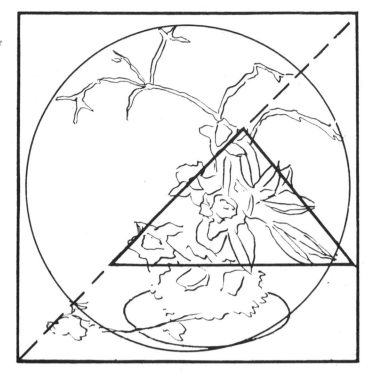

The graphic arts, of which flower arrangement is definitely a member, are governed by eight underlying principles:

DESIGN
SCALE
BALANCE
HARMONY
REPETITION
RHYTHM
ACCENT OR FOCAL POINT
UNITY

In addition, flower arrangement, in common with architecture, must also take a ninth important factor into consideration, and that is

TEXTURE

I shall now deal with each of these principles in turn, explaining their function and application in works of art in general and in flower arrangement in particular.

COMPOSITION

Design   *Scale*   *Balance*

The composition of any work of art is dominated by the principles of design, scale and balance.

Design

Design is the plan or shape of a composition as a whole, and good design must of necessity contain scale and balance. Think for a moment about the building of St. Paul's Cathedral. It was not thrown together haphazardly, without thought. It was first imagined — visualised — before the master plan was finally born in the mind's eye of Christopher Wren. Site and function were taken into consideration, as well as the vitally important question of suitable (and obtainable) materials. Only when these questions had been answered could the basic plan be committed to paper.

A flower arrangement must be planned in exactly the same fashion. Let us say you have gathered a varied assortment of flowers and foliage. What is your ultimate aim? Do you want to create a round arrangement, a half-moon, an S-bend (commonly known as the Hogarth line of beauty), a fan shape, or a peaceful, sweeping horizontal movement? It if is to be created purely for your own pleasure and not for show purposes, a sketch is not absolutely essential. But the shape you desire to achieve must first be visualised. Picture your plan clearly in your mind and then relate that plan — first to the site and function, then to the materials at your disposal.

SITE AND FUNCTION

In show displays you are given the necessary dimensions to which you are to work, thus deciding the question of site and function. In an arrangement created for home use, site and function will be closely related to purpose. For example, you are planning a centrepiece for your dinner table. An arrangement in the round is obviously required, so that it can be viewed with delight on all sides by contented diners. It should also be small, in order to allow your guests a free view of each other. On the other hand, you may want to create a decorative arrangement to be placed in your drawing-room or in a foyer. It will require to be much larger and more lavish, and you must also take into consideration the fact that it will be viewed mainly from the front.

THE MATERIALS

This term includes both the living flowers (buds, berries, branches, foliage etc.) and the container (vase, bowl or other receptacle) which holds them. Both play an equally vital part in your composition. Indeed, one or the other will actually inspire your ultimate design, as can be seen in the photographs and diagrams on page 13.

In general it can be said that the choice of the container is the most important. Select it first, and then find the living materials to complement it. This is the only way to ensure 100 per cent succes, and certainly in show work it is absolutely essential.

However, there are times when the seasons themselves will dictate your choice. During the bounteous summer, with such a rich variety of living materials at hand, you can experiment with many types of new and unusual containers. In the winter months, when flowers are scarce and expensive, the flowers will inspire your design and the container will perforce take second place.

This, however, does not mean that in such circumstances you will not be able to achieve a very beautiful arrangement. To return for a moment to the analogy of St. Paul's. At the time of building it, Wren had a limited amount of Portland stone at his disposal. It had been only recently discovered, and was thought to be in short supply. He finally overcame his difficulties by supporting the inside of St. Paul's famous dome with piers which were themselves filled with rubble!

An all-round arrangement, planned for a dinner party, and designed to suit a round or square dinner table. For use in a dominantly blue coloured dining-room, it consists of pink tulips, blue iris and hyacinths, with touches of white narcissus. Held in a silver compote dish, neutral grey-green foliage hides the pinholder and wire netting. The iris leaves are used on their reverse, thus revealing their delightful silver linings. They are fashioned into 'bows' and set as graceful 'fillers' lower in the design. All-round arrangements are somewhat more difficult to execute, because every facet of the design is on view. Concise instructions to aid both beginners and advanced flower arrangers will be found on pages 72—84

its principles, lack of scale is certain to call forth a negative response. By the same token, a pleasing work of art will immediately excite a positive reaction of appreciation and pleasure. We can sum up our initial reaction in three words — we say 'It looks right' or 'It looks wrong'. This first fleeting judgment of the eye can be your primary guide to an awareness of scale.

As you investigate the subject more deeply, you will discover that the elusive quality of *proportion* is closely linked with scale. This is as true of flower arrangements as any form of artistic expression, and without continuous reference to both success cannot be achieved.

To sum up, we can say that scale can be defined as meaning the size relationship of the component parts of a composition, involving at all times a due sense of proportion between flowers, foliage, container, site and function.

Scale

We now come to the second principle of design in art. Its function is self-explanatory. For example, imagine what a useless document a map would be if it were drawn without reference to scale. What a very peculiar house one would build if this were not taken into consideration! You might well find the windows placed halfway through the first floor, and the doorway so low that it would be almost impossible to squeeze inside.

In exactly the same way, a work of art undertaken without due reverence for scale will not only fail to fulfil its function, but will also be offensive to the eye. Whether or not your audience has an appreciation of knowledge of art and

THE WRONG WAY
The chrysanthemums within the goblet are out of scale with the other flowers

A lead container here holds grey stemmed mauve-tinted seed heads of ornopordum, and silver-grey and lilac-tinted acanthus flower bracts. The fresh leaf head from a pineapple makes a striking focal point. All stems are held on a pinholder which is assisted by a cage placed over the pins

This natural-coloured gypsy basket of tawny and yellow chrysanthemums and golden privet is an example of the proper scale relationship between flowers, foliage and container

Correct form balance: daffodils, tulips and graceful foliage in a charming curved dish are an excellent example of the beauty of a balanced design

Below
Incorrect form balance: The 'shadow' flowers on the right of the central candle help to put this design into correct form-balance. But without the shadows the arrangement would be incorrectly balanced, because there would be too much weight to the left of the candle

Balance

The two essential components of balance are form and colour, and they must be closely related at all times.

FORM

Form falls into one of the two following general categories:

1. Where balance is achieved by the weight being equally distributed on either side of an imaginary central line.

2. Where balance is achieved by conveying a visual effect of equal weight, even though both sides are irregular in form or shape.

COLOUR

When colour is used in either of the two above categories it will do much to aid and enhance the effect of balance. Depth and brightness of colour will provide weight and anchorage, particularly when counterbalanced by a plentiful use of the more delicate tones and shades.

Here are contrasting examples of excellent form-balance, perfectly achieved between materials and container

Above: a pyramid of anemones and eucalyptus leaves are the perfect complement to the pretty container

Left: a spring design, in which polyanthus, narcissi and primroses form a graceful asymmetrical triangle in a lead container. This is known as a cut-and-growing arrangement as the primroses and polyanthus are still in soil, and can be eventually returned to the garden

It is essential, however, that colour should not be used as though it were confetti, scattered here and there without set purpose in the overall design. If employed in this way it will distract and bewilder the beholder, immediately calling forth the 'it-looks-wrong' reaction.

On the other hand the correct use of colour, with depth and lightness flowing into one another will immediately result in an admiring 'it-looks-right' response. Indeed it can succeed in so transforming an inferior design that the arrangement may achieve the prize bench, even though lacking in other necessary qualities. A correct colour pattern, when used in proper conjunction with other vital principles of design, scale, and form-

balance, will call forth such a response from the senses that it will be irresistible.

HARMONY

Harmony can be described as summing up all the essentials of form, with particular emphasis on the use of colour. It aims at avoiding all jarring notes. It ensures that the materials used are suitably related — aristocratic lilies linked with the more exotic types of foliage, marigolds from the cottage garden mingling happily with hedgerow materials. It also makes certain that the container is chosen with an eye to both materials and suitability to place and occasion.

Just one bunch of blue iris and pussy willow, showing a very definite rhythm and repetition of line. Stems are held on a pinholder hidden beneath the moss

Repetition

This is nature's very own medium of emphasis — branch after branch of a tree burgeoning with similar leaves, the sea with its succession of dancing waves or threatening rollers — each is symbolic of movement and vibrant life, each suggests patterns and repetitions to be borrowed and used. But go gently with this particular medium. A little repetition in colour or form is intriguing, but an overdose can prove fatal to the best composition.

A royal blue glass dish, containing early red tulips which are effectively complemented by the graceful red dogwood branches

Rhythm

This can best be descrived as a sense of movement which flows through the main lines of any work of art, whether it be a flower arrangement, a picture, or a building. Its purpose is to direct your eye so that the shape of the whole composition is followed and absorbed, your attention held throughout, and your gaze irrevocably drawn back to rest at the focal point (see next page).

This rhythmic movement, which is present in all successful design, prevents any visual distraction when viewing the picture as a whole.

A graceful movement set in motion by the curving stems of the Japanese variegated lonicera, followed by the sturdier flowers of kalanchoe blossfeldiana and three dahlias in an attractive shallow dish

The crescent is a shape of great beauty, and here it follows the sweep of the dolphin, making an effective play upon repetitive line. Rosemary and aucuba foliage, freesias and tulips are used in fashioning, with the tulips emphasising the focal point

Focal point

Here lies the heart and source of all movement, the point at which the artist commences creation, and from which the ebb and flow of rhythmic movement is directed. This focal point may, with discretion, be emphasised either more or less. For example, the necessary accent could be provided by a replica in miniature of the over-all pattern of the composition: an asymmetrical triangle happily containing a repetitive triangle formed by some dominant leaves at the heart of the arrangement, or a pyramid design (symmetrical triangle) with a repetitive pyramid of colour.

Do remember, however, that great care should be taken not to overdo this all-important accent otherwise the effect will become very hard and unattractive.

Unity

You will have noticed that the use of repetition, rhythm and focal point must be soft-pedalled in design. This is for the simple reason that an artistic composition, whether in paints, brick or mortar, or living floral materials, must be all-embracing if it is to be successful. No one factor should be allowed to dominate. It is the arrangement as a whole which should arrest the attention of the beholder. Sudden distracting departures from the main flow or movement must be checked and avoided. For example, a line at a tangent from the main design, or an indiscriminate use of colour, would serve to draw the eye from the picture as a whole.

Texture

This last factor has particular relevance in the art of flower arrangement. Flowers and foliage, like humans, come in markedly different shapes, sizes and types! As a means of fitting them into their proper categories it quite helps to think of them as men and women.

For example, strong-textured, tough leaves like the evergreen laurels, camellia and magnolia leaves, mahonia bealei and the sword-like phormium and yucca, to mention only a few, have a definite quality of robust masculinity. Their ideal partners are to be found in richly feminine flowers such as camellias, magnolias, chrysanthemums and some of the bold hybrid roses, all of which are well defined in shape and possess a strong velvety texture of petal.

On the other hand, less showy, finer-textured evergreens like the golden privet, certain ferns, the gold and silver varieties of elaeagnus, azara (particularly the variety microphylla) and most foliage from the herbaceous border, suggest a quite different masculine quality. They always remind me of trim-hatted city gentlemen, neat and well-groomed. Their most suitable partners are to be found among the daintier roses, narcissi, iris, dahlias and other flowers of a similar type. The very feminine lacy grey-green foliage of cineraria maritima is well suited to the smaller bulbous flowers like muscari and freesias.

My list could go on *ad infinitum* — but it is far better for you to experiment with your own flower combinations, and make your own rewarding discoveries. The great thing to avoid at all times is the marriage of the incongruous — the large and robust, combined with the tiniest and most delicate. Humanly speaking of course, such combinations do occur, and according to one theorist it is a means of ensuring that the human race continues normal development, raising neither giants nor pigmies. Be that as it may — in flower arrangements it results only in a misalliance.

But enough — you are the artist, you must learn to find your own way through garden and woodland. Memorise the nine principles:

DESIGN
SCALE
BALANCE
HARMONY
REPETITION
RHYTHM
ACCENT OR FOCAL POINT
UNITY
TEXTURE

Carry them with you, entrenched in your subconscious. As you learn through constant practice, they will become your stock-in-trade, lending your fingers speed, so that you will choose without confusion and create without labour, just as the pianist makes his piano speak — seemingly without effort, and without a visible score!

One chrysanthemum, a bract of aucuba foliage and three phormium leaves arranged on a pinholder in an individual casserole dish. Particularly suitable for a man's desk, in its simplicity and definition of line

3. *A delicate arrangement of grevillea robusta, beech leaves and dahlias held in a slim brass candlestick. A candlecup holds the arrangement in water*

II YOUR TOOLS – THE MECHANICS OF THE ART

Confidence acquired through perfect craftsmanship leaves the artist free to be creative

Just as a firm and unwavering self-confidence is the essential ingredient of any important achievement, so in flower arrangement ultimate success literally depends upon the strength of the original foundation. The arrangement must hold together firmly. It should be sufficiently well constructed to withstand being moved from room to room, or even from house to house. I have actually taken an arrangement all the way from Devon to a flower show in Chelsea and, even after the long car journey, very little last-minute touching up has been required.

To achieve a proper foundation for your arrangements you must have the right tools and you must know how to use them. In the next few pages you will find all the essential equipment for successful flower arranging described in words and sketches. Some of these tools are necessary to all arrangements, some only to special ones.

A PLASTIC BUCKET

This is much more practical to carry round the garden than the more ornamental trug. If it is partially filled with water, the freshly cut stems of flowers and foliage will, owing to this considerate early drink, last much longer. This is especially true of anemones, polyanthus, lupins, delphiniums etc., whose stems should be recut under water to prevent air bubbles forming and choking these thirsty drinkers. Some species of material require further specialist treatment, such as burning, crushing of stems, or immersion in very hot water (see Chapter VI, which deals with the preservation of materials).

SCISSORS

A good pair of 'Fedco' serrated-edge flower scissors is essential. The serrated edge helps to crush the fibres at the point of severance, enabling the stem to take up more water. The other edge is sharp and is used to scrape the bark of woody stems such as chrysanthemums and all shrubs. These scissors also incorporate an essential wire-cutting groove.

HAMMER AND ANVIL

A small wooden mallet and a chunk of brick or concrete will enable you to deal satisfactorily with those woody branches and stems which require crushing before use (see Chapter VIII).

BORAX

A pinch of borax in the water will not hurt the flowers and foliage, and will do much to offset rusting of the metal pinholders and wire netting.

'TWISTITS'

These are short pieces of wire, encased in green paper covering. They may occasionally be used to hold a difficult stem, in addition to the ordinary wiring in the holder or container. *They must never be visible.*

OLD SHEETING OR CURTAINING

This is necessary to spread on the floor when working, to prevent messing and staining.

LEMONADE STRAWS

These are very useful to replace broken stems or lengthen short ones. Hollow stems of other flowers (e.g. daffodils) will serve the same purpose. The too short or broken stem is inserted into the end of the host stem or straw. When the host stem is placed in the water, capillary action feeds the short stem, enabling it to live as well as if it reached down to the water itself.

SPECIMEN TUBES OR VASES

Use these to lift short-stemmed materials to high places when required in moderately large arrangements.

DETERGENTS

A certain chemical incorporated in the manufacture of one detergent, Tide, makes it particularly useful for dried arrangements (such as Christmas wreaths etc.), which require no water. Mix approximately 2 tablespoons of water with a large cup of Tide (the final consistency should be like a precooked Christmas pudding). Place this mixture in your container, without using any pinholder or wire, and immediately start on your composition. You have about one hour in which to complete the design, after that the Tide sets hard as a rock and the 'everlasting' arrangement is ready, either for immediate admiration or to be put away under tissue paper until required. Tide can also be used in place of Selastik or Plasticine to 'set' a candlecup in a candlestick or any other such combination. It will last perhaps a year before it requires re-doing, and it is very easy to get rid of this home-made 'cement' once an arrangement has fulfilled its purpose. A strong tug will be enough to remove all stems, glass baubles, cones etc. (these can be saved for use again, see Chapter VI). Immerse the container in warm water, and you will soon have a bowlful of detergent, ready for washing, as well as a sparklingly clean container!

WALL DISPLAY CANISTERS

These can be bought, or you can use a home-made contrivance. Their purpose is to enable you to place lighter and usually shorter-stemmed materials very high in a very big arrangement. Church decorations, arrangements created for receptions, or the foyer of a hotel often require these canisters. They must be hung from some of the taller branches or strong stems already being

Candlecup into candlestick

used, or from the wall, if the arrangement is so placed. They are, of course, filled with an independent supply of water.

PLASTICINE

Either use Plasticine or a non-hardening putty like Selastik which is obtainable from builders' merchants. Ironmongers may offer you another variety, looking exactly like a tube of toothpaste both in the pack and in use, but it will not do. Always use Selastik or Plasticine and be sure it is used dry. Press the Plasticine, with *dry hands*, on to a *dry* surface. Then press the pinholder into it, thus firmly combining both container and pinholder. In very cold weather, warming your hands, leaving the Plasticine near heat, or placing it in a warmed dry container will help to make it stick. Once this has been achieved, cold water may be poured in, and the arrangement created. Remember that the base of your container must be level, or the pinholder will wobble, and your arrangement will be insecure. Selastik or Plasticine helps to fill in such curved, moulded or generally uneven containers. It is essential for all mobile arrangements to prevent them toppling in transit. Also, placed in the aperture of a candlestick and pressed in firmly with warm dry hands, it will securely hold a candlecup fitment. Selastik and Plasticine will hold for months on end. However, if you want to transfer your arrangement from one container to another, it can be released by a firm but gentle pulling, or by application of a little hot water, followed by a pull. You can at this point separate your Selastik or Plasticine from the pinholder, or leave them together and transfer the whole unit.

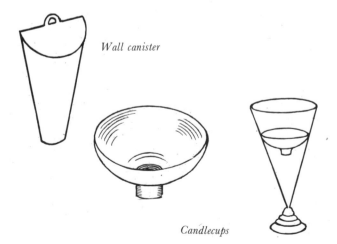

Wall canister

Candlecups

CANDLECUPS

These moderately priced metal cups are obtainable from most florists. Of gold or steel-coloured alloy, they are made primarily, as the name indicates, for use with candlesticks or candelabra. However, they are also very useful as water-holders for other long-stemmed bases. For instance, you may have a delightful figurine or ornamental jug in china, pottery or metal which you long to use in conjunction with flowers. Providing there is a cupped or hollow area at the top (or somewhere near it), you can easily do this by pressing in either Selastik, Plasticine or Tide, then firmly inserting your candlecup. A candlecup can also be successfully combined with a piece of driftwood or a log by once again tucking its base or projection into a hollow lined with Selastik or Plasticine. It can also be used to convert an extremely narrow-necked vessel (e.g. a Persian vase, which normally would be almost impossible to use for flowers). All you need to do is to put a ring of whatever adhesive material you are using around the middle circumference of the candlecup, and then press it into the top of the vase, making sure the adhesive ring is sticking firmly to its rim.

Candlecups are a great aid to good arranging, because they are comparatively shallow. It is therefore much easier to set your stems exactly where you need them, and at precisely the right angles to achieve the lines and curves you require for your design.

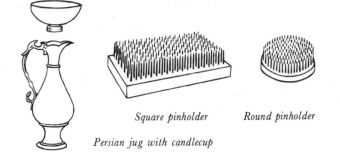

Persian jug with candlecup   *Square pinholder*   *Round pinholder*

HERE ARE THREE IMPORTANT POINTS TO REMEMBER WHEN USING CANDLECUPS

1. Make sure all areas, including your hands, are *absolutely dry*. Selastik or modelling clay will not adhere otherwise.
2. Choose your sticking medium to blend in colour with the base, so as to render the join as unobtrusive as possible. It may be necessary to paint it over lightly.
3. Colour the candlecup so that it is in complete harmony with the base you are using. If this is not possible, design your composition so that the candlecup will be completely hidden, which is rather more difficult to achieve.

PINHOLDERS AND WIRE NETTING

These tools are of equal importance and, though there are times when they are used separately, most arrangements benefit from their being used together. *Always* use pinholders and wire netting in combination in the following containers:

1. Containers which are flat and shallow in shape.
2. Containers which only have a very shallow water-holding area, even though the container itself may be tall stemmed.
3. Any container whose base is large enough to accommodate both netting and pinholder. The wire netting, incidentally, should be at least $1\frac{1}{2}$-inch mesh (not smaller) and as fine a gauge as possible, so that it can be easily squeezed in your hands, inserted in a container or put on a pinholder.

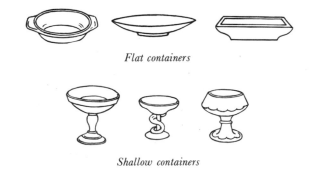

Flat containers

Shallow containers

One branch of spruce fir and just six red tulips with their own foliage make this graceful (complementary coloured) arrangement. They are held in the narrow neck of a Persian metal water jug

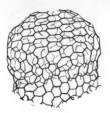

Wire netting   *Pinholders*

Pinholders are used alone, without wire, for Japanese flower arrangements. Indeed, the Japanese traditionally avoid the use of artificial aids. Therefore when you are creating an arrangement in the beautiful Japanese style you must not fix your pinholder to the base of the container with any type of adhesive. This is considered entirely unethical. However, if a situation arises where the pinholder, or *kenzan*, does require help, the solution is as follows. If you need more weight to balance some top-heavy flowering branches, the usual method is to place another smaller pinholder on top of the first. The pins grip each other, thus supplying the necessary extra weight. Some other types of arrangement look better without wire netting. They are actually based on the Japanese tradition, and are usually water designs modelled on the Moribana school of Japanese arrangement. They are characterised by the use of a few materials placed in a shallow container.

With regard to the pinholder itself, the Japanese do not always bother to conceal it as we do, because they do not consider it particularly ugly. We like to continue the theme by using pebbles, shells, attractive fungi or moss, or even lumps of washed coal. In a black container, the latter looks most effective.

Wire netting is used alone in containers which are too awkward in shape to accommodate both it and a pinholder, such as the following:

1. Containers the bottoms of which are so narrow that there is no room for a pinholder.
2. Containers which are so deep that they render the pinholder ineffective, except in relation to the very longest stems.

3. Very small containers, such as wineglasses, or containers so shallow that they would not hold enough water to submerge a pinholder, thus starving the flowers and foliage.
4. Candlecups, if used in conjunction with a candle, although a 1-inch diameter baby pinholder can be used on occasion.

When choosing your pinholder buy the heaviest one you can find. Pinholders consist of a lead and alloy base which is studded with brass or steel 'pins'. There are three of four proprietary makes on the market, some heavier, some lighter; and, of course, the larger the pinholder the greater the length of the pins. It is imperative that flower and foliage stems, and all living materials impaled on the pins, are submerged in at least $\frac{3}{4}$ to 1 inch of water, preferably 2 to 4 inches. Therefore the actual water-holding part of any container must be deep enough to allow for this. In other words, the larger the pinholder the deeper the water-holding area must be. Its depth should be judged in relation to the pins which, at least, should be well awash. For example, a round pinholder measuring $3\frac{1}{2}$ inches in diameter is usually 1 inch in depth (including both base and pins). The container in which it is placed should therefore be capable of containing at least 2 to 3 inches of water, preferably more. Of course, if you are using Plasticine to hold the pinholder firmly, or to level the container's base, this will naturally add to the height of the pinholder. It is not necessary to use a wastefully large amount of Plasticine, but even a small amount will increase the pinholder's height, and that extra height must be allowed for. The best rule to keep in mind is to make sure that the pins are always well covered with water. Once you have chosen the correct container, and firmly fixed the pinholder inside with whatever adhesive you are using (keeping everything dry), you are ready to add the wire netting. As mentioned before, this should be pliable and with a mesh of not less than $1\frac{1}{2}$ inches. Cut off a piece of the right size, using the special section of your scissors (see page 21) or, alternatively, a wire cutter. Remember to avoid the selvedge which should be thrown away as it is uncompromisingly hard to handle.

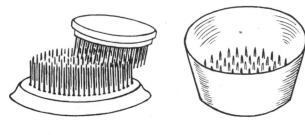

Pinholders   *Well pinholder*

Daffodils and freesia arranged on a pinholder in a hock glass. Two camellias laid on a bed of their own luxurious foliage with heads of sweet scented lilac. Three camellias with a little fern in a wine-glass and three carnations and fern which are literally being kept under glass. Here are three ways which show how a few materials can contribute to many arrangements

JUST HOW MUCH WIRE TO USE?

This is an important question, because so much of the success of your design rests upon using exactly the right amount. Too large a piece will make fitting in all the stems a hopeless task, particularly in a big massed arrangement. On the other hand, too small a piece will mean that the stems will refuse to stay put. To help you attain a happy medium I will provide you with a few approximate measurements. However, remember that they are only relative to the size of the actual water-holding part of your container. They do not apply to its total circumference.

LONG SHALLOW CONTAINER

In these the wire netting is placed directly over the pinholder, leaving the rest of the container clear. You will require a square of netting cut to roughly three times the diameter of the circular pinholder used, in other words, nine times its own area. For example, a 3-inch pinholder requires a square of netting measuring 9 inches by 9 inches.

SHALLOW BOWLS

Again, the wire netting should be placed directly over the pinholder, leaving the remainder of the container clear. The wire should be cut to the same measurements as above, using the size of the pinholder as your yardstick.

CYLINDRICAL OR ELONGATED CONTAINERS

These are the types without false bottoms, in which both water and wire netting can reach all the way to the base. Roll the container in sufficient wire to encircle it with a slight overlap. Allow about a quarter more on the length. Should there be a false bottom this must be taken into account and a shorter length used. Then cork-screw the cylinder of netting and crumple it into the interior of the container.

DEEP URNS

These should be measured by the same method as above. However, be careful that your measurements exclude the non-water holding stem or handle.

SHALLOW URNS OR CIRCULAR COMPOTE DISHES ETC.

These require a square of netting cut to about $1\frac{1}{2}$ times the size of their diameter. However, this must be varied and increased, depending upon the depth of the bowl.

DEEP RECTANGULAR AND FAN SHAPED CONTAINERS

These require a piece of netting cut to their shape, and measuring $1\frac{1}{4}$ times the length by $1\frac{1}{4}$ times the width. This measurement could be increased by another $\frac{1}{4}$ if the container has considerable depth.

The above measurements should provide sufficient wire netting to allow, once the netting is crumpled down, enough layers to hold the individual stems very firmly. With some designs the wire netting takes the place of the pinholder altogether. In others, even when a pinholder is being used, those stems which are to be placed at $75°$ angles, or horizontally, should be 'knitted' into the netting and not impaled on the pinholder.

NOTE: Weave the stems in, through two or three loops of meshed wire, exactly as if you were knitting. This is an essential manoeuvre in the placing of acutely angled or horizontal stems. It is also the only way of ensuring that the stem will stand firm exactly where it is placed.

TO SECURE WIRE NETTING

There are various ways of fixing or holding wire netting firmly in place. Treating the whole container as though it were a sort of parcel and tying the netting into position is the most elementary. However, I seldom subscribe to this method, and then only for large pedestal or mantelpiece arrangements. With such designs it is a means of playing extra safe, and also the telltale string can be hidden by the fall of material. I know it is said that the string can be cut and removed once the arrangement is made, but I have never known a devotee of this method with the courage to do so!

A much better solution is to buy a packet of strong rubber bands. Choosing the most suitable colour and size, place a band around the most convenient and unobtrusive section of your container — for example, the stem directly below the bowl of a wineglass or goblet, or under the outcurving rim of an urn. Then pull the band up and loop it on to a cut end of wire at two or four opposite points. The rubber band should blend with the colour of the container and therefore be almost invisible. Even so it must be hidden by a suitable fall of flower and leaf, and this question should be reckoned with when you are planning your design. On the other hand, if the container you are using has an incurving rim your problems are solved. Once the wire netting has been slipped firmly under this rim it will stay in position without further worry. Ornamental handles or filigree work near the mouth of the container can also be used as an aid to anchorage. In this case, all you need to do is to hook a cut end of wire around the projection.

Much the best method of wiring for all containers is to press the wire down firmly on to the pins of the pinholder, knit the first three stems through the two or three layers of crumpled wire, and then impale them on the pinholder. The method is much the same as the way in which a woman anchors her hat to her head by weaving the hatpins through her hair. It is of particular importance with large shallow containers in which the wire netting only covers the pinholder.

Always crumple the wire with the cut ends, or outside edges, facing upwards (as shown in the sketches on this page). Thus you always have a number of ends available to help deal with recalcitrant stems. It is always an advantage to twist one such cut end of wire around the base of the first stem, which is usually the most important and the longest in the composition, thus giving it extra support. Another valuable use for

Using wire netting (1)

these cut ends is to press them down gently upon a curved stem, so that they hold it and prevent it from straightening, as some flowers are prone to do when put in water. The gentle pressure will not hurt the flowers and will keep them firmly in place. This is a great asset when dealing with such flowers as tulips or anemones. Cut wire-ends also help to hold firm horizontal or severely angled stems which cannot be impaled on the pinholder.

I may appear to be over-emphasising the question of wiring. However, you must remember that correct wiring (with or without the pinholder) is the foundation of the whole structure. No worthwhile design can ever be achieved with a makeshift, insecure foundation. If you have ever been called upon to judge, as I have, a once-lovely arrangement that has become a casualty because of a faulty foundation, you will appreciate why I am being so emphatic. First give your arrangement a good foundation and then the rest will follow — this being the basis of all successful flower arrangement.

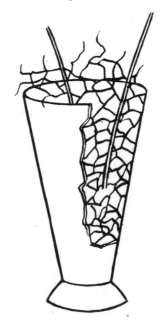

Using wire netting (2)

Right: Placing of stems in wire netting. Far right: fine stems, lashed to thicker one for support, can be impaled on pinholder.

The combined use of wire netting and pinholder will meet the requirements of all types of materials. However, there are certain points to be kept in mind. Fleshy stems, such as anchusa and anemones, prefer sitting clear of the pinholder, and should be held by the netting alone. Hard materials, such as the stalks of shrubs and chrysanthemums, are better impaled on the pins of the pinholder, as this helps their intake of water, as well as securing them more firmly. Very delicate spidery stems will not impale successfully, and should be knitted into the netting. If they are excessively fine, like rockery sedums and the ornamental fancy grasses, it is better to concentrate a few in one spot by lashing the delicate stems on to a piece of woody stem. Make sure that all stem ends reach the base of this stake or host stem, and then impale it on to the pinholder.

PARAMOUNT FLOWER HOLDERS

These are useful accessories and can be used instead of pinholders, or in conjunction with them, with perhaps the addition of a little wire netting. The latter should only be a fractional piece, just tucked between the two layers of the superstruc-

ture, with a few cut ends projecting at the top. Paramount holders can only be used successfully in a container with a completely level bottom. Otherwise their three rubber suction pads will not be able to keep a firm grip on the container. Unlike Selastik or Plasticine, they must be used wet and placed on a wet surface or they will not hold.

Paramount holder   *Cage*

CAGES

These are very useful indeed. Made in three sizes to fit neatly over most round pinholders, they take the place of wire netting. They are especially useful when creating dinner-table arrangements in open, shallow containers.

MARBLES, PEBBLES, SHELLS, GRANITE PIECES, COAL

All of these can be used most effectively, not only to hold stems in glass containers, but also to camouflage ungraceful stalks; to conceal the pinholder and wire netting or to form a 'built-up' container. Indeed, by choosing these accessories in colours which are linked to your main colour scheme, and by an imaginative arrangement of them in your container, you can greatly enhance the beauty of your design.

Arranging flowers without wire or pinholder can present a problem. This happens when visiting friends who ask you to do the flowers but can provide no mechanics or even a suitable container! Here is one quite successful solution. These pale blue Wedgwood and darker blue Vanfleet iris are casually arranged in a goblet. Their stems are held in position by pebbles and a little moss placed in the base of the goblet

FLORAPAK

This is a white, cellular substance, light as air, which is stocked by all florists, and sold in various-sized packs. According to the instructions given by the manufacturer, it should be cut to the size and shape of the container, and then pressed into it, so that it is an exact fit. This is easy enough with rectangular or round containers, but somewhat difficult with more unusual shapes. Moreover, after Florapak has been in use for a short time, both water and stems tend to break up the delicate fabric. I would therefore advocate taking a chunk of the material, placing it in a plastic bag, sprinkling a little water in it, then crunching it up until it is pliable enough to pack into the container and hold the stems. Another disadvantage of Florapak is that some flowers do not live long in this medium as it tends to work its way into their stems. Anemones, especially, dislike it intensely. In my opinion, its main use is for short-term, special occasion arrangements, for example a dinner-party composition which is to be arragned in a glass dish or bowl. Florapak makes the use of wire unnecessary, and also effectively conceals the criss-cross underwater stems. Also, it looks quite attractive through the transparent glass and effectively echoes the white of a damask tablecloth. After 24 hours or so, the arrangement should be transferred to another container, in which you utilise either a pinholder or wire, or both. By this means you will enjoy the pleasure of using your lovely cut glass or silver*, safe from possible wire scratches and with stems hidden from view, and of ensuring long life for your flowers. Florapak is also indispensable for miniature compositions. Working with minute materials to small proportions (often under 4 inches as an all-over measurement), it would be impossible to use wire or pinholders.

FLORAFOAM

This is another product which looks uncommonly like Florapak, but is no relation. It is of firm, cellular texture and cannot be used in conjunction with water. Although it is no use for living arrangements, it can be used to advantage for dried and artificial Christmas decorations (see Chapter VI) either within the container or, in fact, acting as the container itself. The materials used with it have to have either strong stiff stems, or be mounted on wire. It is useful too for cut-outs.

OASIS

This is one of the latest of the mechanical aids to arrangement. It is also of a spongy cellular nature and is used either in blocks or pressed into the shape of your container. It retains moisture for a considerable time and the stems seem to thrive in it. I derive great satisfaction from its use whenever I have an awkwardly shaped container, or only the centre of a very shallow dish, at my disposal. Of course, it can also be used instead of wire netting in the deeper containers, if desired. However, one cannot use the same piece too often, and this makes it somewhat expensive.

* Note: When using any adhesive such as putty or Selastik on silver or plate, do not leave it in position for more than 36 hours at the outside or staining of the metal will result. When working with silver it is actually more advisable to use either a second inner container or a polythene lining, and create your arrangement in this.

4. *Anemones have a habit of huddling together after arrangement. Prevent this by using a generous amount of foliage. Senecio greyii, used here, makes an attractive neutral foil for these gay flowers*

5. *During winter you need not restrict your design by the length of your longest flower; utilise a branch, such as this lichen-covered apple bough, to set the line. The few chrysanthemums and pernettya berries are partnered with their foliage*

6. *A fresh-looking arrangement for which I used crisp yellow-green hydrangea leaves, yellow ranunculus, Esther Read chrysanthemums and delicate lily of the valley, arranged in a diagonal line based upon the shape and colour of the artistic dolphin container* (Photograph courtesy of 'Woman')

7. *Good line repeated by a skilful blending of colours is as necessary in a pot plant arrangement as it is for cut flowers and foliage. The little extra trouble I took in planting these arrangements in compost (instead of wire netting) is well repaid by the extra weeks of pleasure derived from both lovely compositions*

On the left, the strong lines of tall sansevieria and the flowing green and white hedera, peperomia magnoliaefolia and cryptanthus tri-color combine with colourful dracaenas, Rex begonias and flaming red and snow-white cyclamen and poinsettia in flower. Placed in an earthenware bowl which is held within the attractive wrought iron stand, they make a colourful Christmas decoration

On the right, a pyramid arrangement in a pedestal vase utilises a tall hedera for the main proportionate line, followed by yellow and pink crotons flanking three calamondins. A forward-flowing hoya breaks the hard rim of the container, and softens the general effect of the design

(Photograph courtesy of Rochford's House Plants)

III THE PERSONAL ART OF FLOWER ARRANGING

How do I begin? Understanding what you do and why is halfway to perfection

The moment has come to begin to put all this theory into practice! You are faced with a vase, some flowers and some foliage. What are you going to do? Just put all the materials into the container, not troubling to attempt anything more than making sure the stems touch the bottom so the flowers have a drink? No architect ever built a house that way! At this stage, you will have assembled all your necessary tools, the physical ones as well as the mental equipment acquired by our growing knowledge of both principles and craftsmanship. You are now ready to begin the exciting experience of building your first truly creative flower arrangement, and to study the *five basic practical rules* which govern all flower arranging.

Firstly, look at your materials. Lay them out on the table beside you, to be able to see them. Place the tall, slender-budded stems and branches on one side, and the shorter, bushier rounded materials on the other. Sort them out according to colour as well; the heavier, darker-colour flowers and foliage together, with the elegant, spiky and preferably lighter colours beside them.

Now study your container. You probably have quite a few vases which might go well with your flowers and foliage, and remembering what I said in Chapter I, you already will have brought a very critical eye to the selection of this most important part of your flower-picture. Just as you would not dream of wearing heavy brogue shoes with a cocktail dress, you will not choose a sturdy, heavy-textured, dark-coloured pottery bowl to use with light-textured, dainty materials like larkspur, or filigree silvery-grey foliage like cineraria maritima. If you have a pottery bowl you will wisely keep it to use with strong evergreen and tough chrysanthemums. For daintier materials you will choose an alabaster-type urn or a delicate natural shell. However, remember that the aim should be to achieve a light effect, since all containers must be comparatively weighty and very well balanced for stability (you will find

Forced sprays of forsythia, daffodils in full flower and bud, and paper-white narcissus, arranged in an asymmetrical triangle with holly and conifer. A design which seems to epitomise the promise of spring while winter still lingers

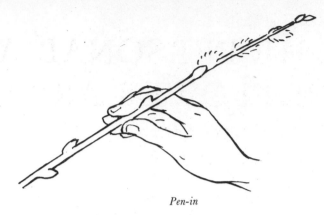

Pen-in

a whole chapter devoted to containers (pages 131—144). Of course you already know that the colour of the container must complement the flowers and foliage with which it is to be combined. Finally, both the flowers and the container must be in complete harmony and unity with the particular surroundings in which the arrangement is to be set.

As you begin work, remember that the outlines of any design are created by the lighter spiky forms of foliage and flowers, by lightly berried branches and especially by the use of buds. This applies to both heavily and delicately textured materials within their own floral categories. In a heavy arrangement for example, in which perhaps laurels, rhododendrons or gladioli were being used, your light material could be very tightly furled gladioli. You would choose these for the tallest main stems which would set the outline of the design. Similarly, in a light-textured arrangement the main stem could be clarkia, larkspur or a sprig of grey-green rosemary foliage, used perhaps in conjunction with the more solid shapes and textures of roses, Achillea, etc. With certain exceptions, which are explained in detail in the chapter on colour, the paler tints of colour combine best with these lighter forms (see Texture, page 18, and also colour plates 13, 17).

Once the outline of the composition is set,

fill in the design by working downwards and inwards from the terminals or outlines, using the comparatively heavier-looking shapes of flowers and foliage. Work in an in-and-out movement which I express as 'pen-in' and 'dart-out' (see diagrams).

Pen-in means that you hold the stems as you would a pen or pencil when writing. This tends to place them in the container at more upright angles. These pen-in stems provide the recession or depth of your design.

Dart-out indicates that you should hold the stems of your materials while placing them in the container as if you were about to throw them at a dartboard. They tend to be set at more outward flowing angles, which provide relief or contrast to the pen-in stems, thus avoiding a flat and uninteresting face to your 'flower-picture'.

The use of colour in flower arranging and the many types and varieties of possible colour schemes are discussed in detail in Chapter V. However, there are a few points which should also be mentioned here. Increase the intensity of colour, tone and strength of form as you descend toward the centre, or until the climax is reached at the focal point of your design. This may be emphasised either by a strong rounded form and an increased depth of colour, or conversely by a dash of light colour surrounded by dark rich foliage and berries.

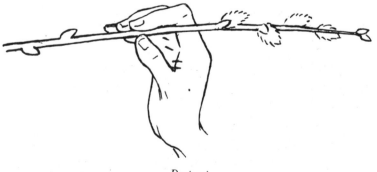

Dart-out

Three variegated phormium leaves and some scarlet anemones, packed into the bottle mouth, stay firm by themselves. An excellent example of good scale and proportion

The Rules

1. MEASURE YOUR CHOSEN CONTAINER

You require to know its greatest diameter if the container is long or round, its greatest height if it is tall. This measurement, plus half again, is the minimum visual measurement for your main stem and establishes the finished height of your arrangement. It may, for certain styles of composition, be much longer, but never less. Otherwise your arrangement will sadly lack the proportion and scale so essential to good design. Always remember, when cutting that first vital stem, that you must allow for the extra amount which will disappear into the container.

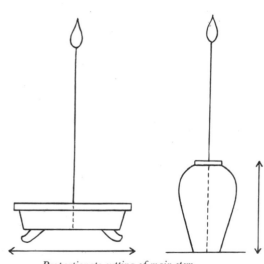

Proportionate cutting of main stem

Wrong container

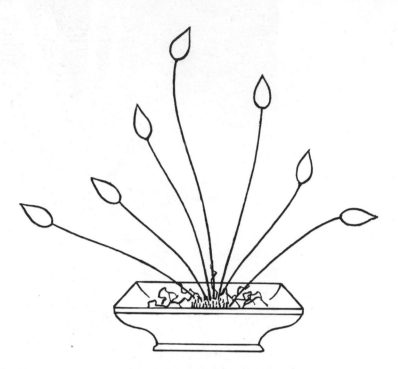

THE RIGHT WAY

2. CENTRALISE THE STEMS

Every stem must spring from the one centre of your composition, from its focal point, or you will not achieve a sense of unity. Keep the picture of a wheel in your mind's eye. Remember how all the spokes return to or spring from the hub. When the spoke breaks away from the hub, how ugly it looks! Exactly the same principle applies in a painting or flower arrangement in which the spokes are the rhythmic and repetitive lines. A tree with its branches is another example.

NOTE: In the creation of a long, flat arrangement in which most of the stems are short the stems which are to be placed at the most horizontal angle need not touch the centre so long as they are positioned in such a way as to give the necessary visual impression of unity.

THE WRONG WAY

THE RIGHT WAY

3. VARY YOUR STEM LENGTHS

Cut them in such a way that no major materials stand shoulder to shoulder or directly above each other, thereby forming a straight line. Precision and orderliness may be much admired in the Army, but will not, in this case, attract the artistic eye.

Vary the heights of your flowers and dominant foliage as you place them in your arrangement. This is the proper method of throwing your design into relief.

THE WRONG WAY

THE RIGHT WAY

4. AVOID CROSSED STEMS

To be more precise, avoid them where they will be visible. There are certain exceptions to this rule which are discussed in Chapter VII, but on the whole when crossing of stems does occur it should be under the water level of the container. Great care should be taken with the placing of the main lines of your composition. Particular attention should be paid to trimming branches, flowering shrubs and bushy materials, to avoid a tangled hedge-like look.

THE WRONG WAY

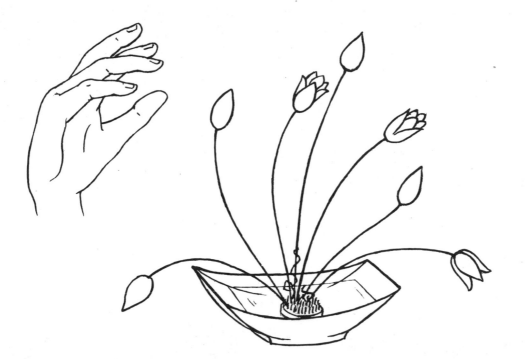

5. LET THE FLOWERS AND FOLIAGE EMBRACE YOUR CONTAINER

Some of you already may have encountered the four rules already given. This fifth rule, although tangible enough and very important, has never previously been stated or expounded as such. However, the need for it to be defined explicitly becomes more obvious with each lesson I give.

To understand precisely what I mean when I talk about flowers embracing a container, try the following experiment. Hold up the palm of your hand, resting your elbow on a table or chair arm. Separate your fingers a little at the same time and very slightly relax or flex your whole hand. Now look at your hand sideways. The curving line which follows from your palm to your slightly outstretched fingers exactly illustrates the slight concave movement which should exist between your container and the materials you place inside it.

The reason why it is essential to create this relationship is that flower arranging, unlike many other arts, requires an all-important third dimension which gives it depth as well as breadth and height. As you fill in your arrangement this effect is enhanced by placing all the stems at different angles, using the pen-in and dart-out movements of your hand.

NOTE: For example, a great painting can make you feel you are actually walking down a street, looking into doorways and round corners. This realistic impression of perspective is conveyed on canvas by the brilliant use of paint. The flower arranger obtains the same effect through practising my fifth rule.

Delicate sprays of golden privet and Esther Read chrysanthemums follow a softly curving diagonal line in repetition of the 'ribbon' held in the hand of the figurine container

Remember when you are creating your flower arrangement it is much better to build it on the spot, where you will be constantly aware of exactly the effect it will have on the table, alcove or mantelpiece it is intended to decorate. Mess and staining can be avoided by an old sheet or curtain kept especially for this purpose, which you can place on the floor under your feet. When the job is finished you just collect all the bits and pieces by bundling the sheet inwards from the corners.

However, if you have to work away from the final location of your arrangement, as when preparing something for a show, you must constantly bear in mind its dimensions in relation to the height of its eventual background. For show work, of course, this is absolutely vital, but really equally important if you want to achieve the best possible effect in your own sitting room.

The method of working to given dimensions for shows, for example creating an arrangement for a 3-foot niche, requires a special technique.

For all the other types of arrangements, all that you need to remember is that any dimensions which you have been given should be regarded as the frame in which your flower-picture will eventually be set. And a well-framed picture is one in which the frame is never allowed to encroach upon the actual painting. Therefore, avoid extending the main lines of an arrangement to the maximum of the measurements indicated. For example, in a 3-foot niche a line arrangement could extend to 2 feet 6 inches, or 2 feet 9 inches at one extremity, but in a mass arrangement it would be best to keep its proportions well within the niche itself.

Now you are ready to go back to your flowers and foliage. As you begin your work allow yourself to be guided by their lovely curves and bends, by all the little idiosyncrasies of their natural growth. Once you have assimilated the foregoing notes, it is these curves and bends which ought to, and will, I am sure, suggest the inspiration for your composition.

8. *A Japanese-style arrangement utilising a minimum of material with the maximum effect. Just three lichen-covered branches and three chrysanthemums, with washed coal to cover the kenzan (pinholder)*

9. *Megasea leaf and some holly, arranged with griselinia foliage, carnations and anemones in a trough*

IV HOW TO BUILD UP DESIGNS

Your own creation — the method may be mine, but the finished picture is yours

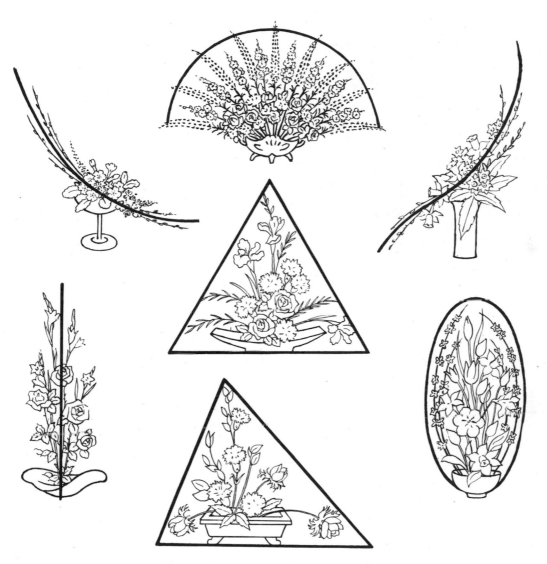

The geometrical shapes created in flower arranging

Since it is not given to everyone to visualise abstract forms easily, I am going to help you get started by working out fourteen different designs with you. In the following pages you will find a detailed description of the 'build-up' of each of these designs, as well as step-by-step marginal sketches. These designs are based upon simple geometrical shapes, but this does not mean you require a course in higher mathematics. You only need to realise that the rules of geometry are our guide to the creation of abstract shapes, from beautiful curves to formal angles. They form the basis for the plans of all architects and all artists.

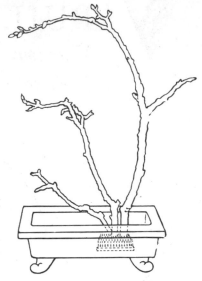

Japanese asymmetrical triangle (1)

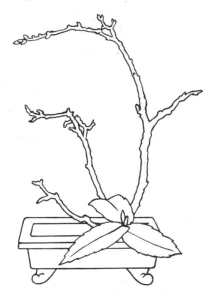

Japanese asymmetrical triangle (2)

For our first design let us arrange two asymmetrical (ueven-sided) triangles, the first in Japanese style, the second in a Westernised version.

The Japanese asymmetrical triangle is perhaps the most aesthetically satisfying of all flower arrangements. It is also one of the easiest shapes to execute, and because its sides are uneven it requires less material than a symmetrical from. Emphasis on quality rather than quantity, a pure, clear realisation of outline, extreme precision and delicacy of execution — these are the ingredients for the successful creation of a Japanese asymmetrical triangle. They are also my definition of a good line arrangement.

The asymmetrical triangle — Japanese style

The basis of all Japanese art is symbolic. In its three main lines it represents Heaven, Man and Earth. These are called respectively *Shin*, *Soe* and *Hikae*. The ancient schools of Japanese flower arrangement were very strict regarding both the choice and the amount of materials used. The modern school, which is the one imitated by the West, allows considerably more freedom. One important rule, however, is that the plant materials used must be those which are natural associates in nature. In other words, flowers, trees and shrubs which grow in a similar environment. For example, irises, hosta leaves and willow branches would be a suitable combination because they reach full leaf and flower at the same time and all love moist or wet ground.

A low, flat container is generally used, with only a pinholder (or *kenzan*, as it is called in Japanese) securing the flowers. The whole container may be filled with water, or the stems may be placed within a small flat vessel, which is itself contained in or placed on an attractive base of some sort.

Shin, representing Heaven, is always the longest and most important line, wherever it may happen to be placed. It generally takes the form of a carefully pruned branch. It must be cut to measure the width of the container, plus its depth and up to half as much again. You should include the base in this measurement, if it is an integral part of the container.

Shin is placed at an angle of 10° off vertical. (In Japanese flower arrangement the Zero line is vertical. Thus 10° is practically upright.) *Shin* should slope slightly forward and be impaled on the back of the pinholder, which is set to one side or the other of the container but never in the centre. A beautiful curving stem with a 'heel', as depicted in the sketch, provides the ideal line for *Shin*.

Soe, representing Mankind, is also chosen for a lovely curve, plus if possible a heel. It is cut to

three-quarters the length of *Shin* and placed at an angle of 45° off vertical and set, so to speak, in the middle distance.

Hikae, representing the Earth, is the shortest line. It is cut to three-quarters the length of *Soe* and is placed at an angle of 75° off vertical. It should be tilted forward and outwards, again utilising graceful curves, all of which should have preferably an upward-tilting tip. This upward tilt suggests happiness, the curve of smiling lips.

The three lines of *Shin*, *Soe* and *Hikae* should be kept together, springing up from the *kenzan* for about 4 inches if possible before breaking into their graceful curves. Hence the importance of the useful heel.

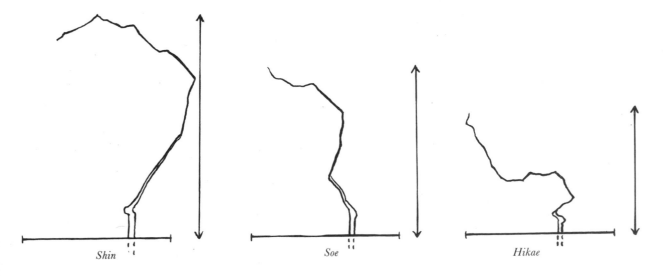

Shin　　　　　*Soe*　　　　　*Hikae*

Three branches of escallonia form the shushis (main lines) of the keishin-kei (windswept) Japanese-type arrangement. Three picture roses form the jushis, or auxiliaries

The *jushis*, which are the additions to these main lines and may consist of either flowers or foliage, are now placed in position. However, not one of them must exceed three-quarters the height of *Shin*, the main stem. After all, no flower grows higher than a tree. Incline the *jushis* slightly to the right and left of centre, following the line indicated by *Shin*, the main stem. If you are using flowers, see that they face slightly off-centre. The Japanese declare it is very rude for anyone, even a flower, to stare you in the face!

Practising even this one arrangement will give you great happiness and will also be of much assistance in any subsequent arrangements you try. It will help you to distinguish between good line and unnecessary frills and to avoid that bugbear of all beginners — overcrowding.

Taking leave of the East, we will now revert to the zero line as represented by the horizontal and, when we undertake our Westernised version of the asymmetrical triangle, we can use all the legitimate aids to arrangement as described in Chapter II in which the tools and mechanics of flower arranging are discussed.

The asymmetrical triangle - Western style

This design may be arranged in a variety of containers; tall, short, flat, or pedestal type — in fact whichever you prefer.

Fix the pinholder firmly in the position dictated by the type of container you are using; that is, centrally in a round one or at one end in an oval or oblong, as shown in the diagrams.

Add water, making sure that the pins of the pinholder are well awash. Secure some $1\frac{1}{2}$-inch wire mesh on top of the pins and then measure your container. Cut your first and tallest stem to equal or exceed the container's largest measurement at least $1\frac{1}{2}$ times, and do not forget to allow a bit extra for that part of the stem which will disappear into the container. Set this stem well back on the pins with a slight backward slope. It is preferable to choose one with a nice curve, though this can be achieved with pliable foliage through a gentle stroking between warm hands. A number of varieties can be made to bend to your will in this fashion, such as broom, some elaeagnus and all types of willow. Arum and other lilies will also oblige, if you tear a strip off the stem on the side you wish to incline. However, beware of brittle stems such as mahonias, berberis, zinnia, and sweet william, as they will not co operate.

Once the main stem is in position, secure it further by twisting an end piece of the wire netting an inch or so up its length. And I would like to emphasise again the importance of achieving a slight backward slope. This helps both visual and actual balance as well as contributing to a three-dimensional effect in the finished design.

Western asymmetrical triangle
See colour plate 9, page 42

The second or complementary stem is cut slightly shorter than the main stem. Place it in position by either impaling it on the pinholder or knitting it into the wire netting. It should be placed at an angle of approximately 20° above or below the horizontal zero line and tilted forward, in order to indicate its affinity with the focal point of your design.

The third stem, which is again shorter than the main one and complementary to the second, is also tilted forward slightly at an angle of approximately 45°. It can be placed either to the right or the left of the main stem (see diagram).

Once these three stems are in position (they may be flowers, foliage or branches) the uneven triangle or 'bones' of your composition have been established. We can now proceed to fill-in.

Western asymmetrical triangle (1)

Western asymmetrical triangle (2)

As you begin the process of filling in, take care never to exceed the outline you have set yourself. You can use buds and spiky forms, with lighter tints placed high in the arrangement. Work downwards, gradually introducing the more solid round shapes and stronger hues, in order to spotlight gently the axis or focal point of a design. Once your flower-picture is complete the eye should be drawn to this point, and from it should move around and through the whole design and then back again to the beginning. In this way a proper sense of rhythm and unity is achieved.

Do not forget to check your arrangement with an imaginary plumb-line held through the centre of the focal point as shown in the photographs which illustrate the principle of balance (page 12).

Since you are now composing an asymmetrical design, balance should be achieved by the distribution of a little heavy-looking material placed low on one side of the imaginary line, with tall, springing material on the other. Is this true of your design? Fine! On the other hand, if it is top-heavy and leaning too much toward the tall side, correct the balance by introducing more weight on the lower side. A dark, round flower or heavy, important leaf bract such as rhododendron or a rosette of the evergreen daphniphyllum should do the trick. If your problem is the reverse, then you should also reverse the solution.

You must make sure that the height of your design is correct and that you have successfully avoided a flat just-trimmed-the-hedge look. This is best prevented at the initial stages of your work by the proper setting and angling (backwards, centrally and forwards) of the three main lines of the design. A further safeguard is the use of the pen-in, dart-out movements when you reach the filling-in stage.

Paper-white narcissus and gay daffodils herald the spring in this version of an asymmetrical triangle

Spring is here! A symmetrical design of yellow daffodils and mimosa, with tawny orange tulips to emphasise the colouring associated with this time of year

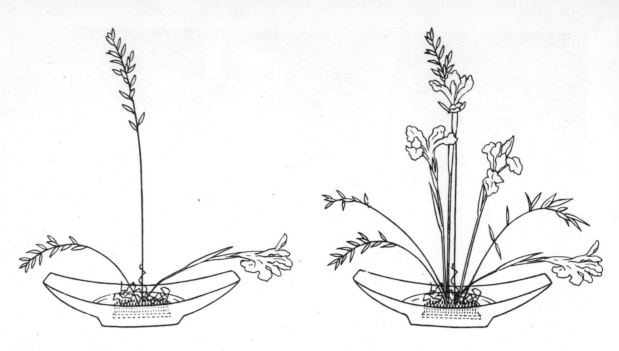

The pyramid (1)   *The pyramid (2)*

The pyramid or symmetrical triangle

This design, since it is symmetrical, and therefore requires equal balancing of the two halves of the picture it presents, is just a trifle more difficult than the asymmetrical shape. It is nevertheless still very simple, and with its several possible variations can be most charming in effect.

Your choice of container can be varied, depending upon which style of triangle you decide to create. The design shown in the diagrams always looks well in any oblong or flattish type of container. It is, however, particularly effective in a cylindrical shape as shown, suggesting the lovely lines of a larch tree, which always reminds me of graceful hands with upturned fingertips beckoning one to behold and admire.

To create this picture ourselves, we must look for some beautifully curving foliage or flowers, perhaps a few delicate branches of the larch tree itself.

Once you have collected your materials, put the pinholder with the wire netting over it in the centre of your chosen container. It must *always* be central for a symmetrical design. Cut your first stem, perhaps an iris, making it the minimum $1\frac{1}{2}$ times the greatest measurement of the container. Preferably, for this type of arrangement,

it should be much longer and can indeed be up to $2\frac{1}{2}$ times the container's largest measurement. Secure this main stem on to the centre back of your pinholder or wire netting, tilting it backwards slightly. Strengthen its position by a twist of wire netting around its stem. The heavier your flower stem is, the greater the need to make sure that this first line is absolutely secure.

Now choose two suitably curved stems of flowers and foliage, or curve some pliable material within your warmed hands. Cut the two stems to an identical length but shorter than the main stem, and set them equidistant from the central stem, one on each side of it. They should be inserted almost horizontally at about 10° from the zero line. Do not forget to incline both of them forwards at the same time, so as to create that all-important three-dimensional look.

Continue the general outline by setting two more supporting stems within the perimeter (see diagram). Then you can proceed to fill in with darker hues and heavier, more solid forms. Finish the design with some subtle touch as the focal point, perhaps a rosette of leaves, resembling a triangle, or some similarly placed contrasting colour.

10.   *The pyramid (3). Glycerine-preserved eucalyptus foliage, blue iris, paper-white narcissus, a bunch of violets and freesias are held in a pinholder in this shallow glazed dish. Leaves conceal the pinholder*

13. To brighten the dullest of days — a pyramid of glowing golden chrysanthemums, yellow freesias, magenta anemones and carnations. With wire netting and pinholder, the flowers are quite simple to arrange in this gilded incense burner

Another example of a symmetrical design. Carnations, gladioli, pompon dahlias and eucalyptus combine happily. A pinholder and wire netting hold the stems firmly within the sturdy compote container

A candlestick or figurine, used in conjunction with a candlecup, offers an attractive variation of the pyramid design. Indeed, you can use any tall container, providing it also has a shallow area holding water, such as the incense burner used in the diagram on the next page.

By making the pyramid slightly more bulgy around its waistline and by dropping the two curving, complementary lines to an acute angle (say 25° below the horizontal line, and also maintaining a slightly forward tilt), you will achieve a pretty weeping tree effect.

The pyramid (3)
See colour plate 13, page 54

The pyramid (1)

Delightful though the weeping tree effect may be, it is always rather tricky to secure stems firmly when they have to be tilted at such very acute angles. However, firm they *must* be, or disaster will overtake your arrangement. If you are able to find curving stems with a right-angled and left-angled heel, your task will be much easier. On the other hand, as is more often the case, you may find you have only a gently curving stem to work with. In these circumstances you will have to rely mainly on firm wiring. Knit your stems through the wire netting, making them additionally secure and also encouraging more curve by using the ends of the wire netting to exert a slight pressure upon them, as shown in the diagram.

These dropping, complementary stems are measured by the height of the container, and can range between half to three-quarters of its length (excluding the curve) but no more. Either side of the perimeter, halfway between the tip of the main stem and the tips of the two complementaries, place two additional curving stems. Cut these long enough to create the bulge, and follow this outline faithfully while filling in. Also bear in mind the fact that the unusual drooping complementaries of this particular design should be treated as terminals and given the 'light touch of colour' treatment. They *must* be prevented from looking ponderous, which can easily happen if they are heavily handled.

The pyramid (2)

A variation of the oval design, with curving white gladioli and grey eucalyptus foliage creating a U-shaping. It is held in a well-pinholder, which is tucked into a piece of drift-wood. Deep blue hydrangeas conceal the base and form a dark-coloured focal point

The oval

During the high summer you may feel like having a big show of flowers, and yet not want to make a particularly large arrangement.

One way of expressing such a mood is to create what is technically known as a *mass design*, which depends upon a great quantity and variety of materials rather than size for its effect. However, it must possess line or it will fail to please.

An oval shape lends itself very well to a mass design, creating a very satisfying arrangement which is also fairly simple to construct.

When choosing a container, try to find one similar to the oval shape you intend to create. A loving cup or a deep rose bowl, placed perhaps on a little platform, would be a good choice. Depicted overleaf is a pottery bowl, slightly raised

on its own little pedestal, making it a fraction higher than it is wide. Thus the measurement for the main stem is taken from the height of the container, which must also include its pedestal base (see diagram).

As usual, when cutting the main stem, you must allow for the length which disappears unseen into the bowl. Therefore it should be cut quite a bit more than the minimum proportion of $1\frac{1}{2}$ times the height of the container. Its measurement should be twice the height, not forgetting to allow for the extra unseen portion. Now, having set the pinholder centrally, and as far back in the container as it will go, thread the main stem through the wire netting, and fix it on to the centre back of the pinholder.

The oval (3)
Gladioli, variegated phormium leaves, peonies, an arum and a kniphofia are here arranged in an oval design

The oval (1)

The oval (2)

even the curly heart of a cos lettuce, which is such a deliciously fresh green. As you work, be very careful to retain the graduated oval outline, and make sure there is plenty of depth in your picture, which you will achieve by the correct angling of your stems, and by placing them with the usual pen-in, dart-out movements. Solid, rounded flowers like roses look particularly effective *en masse* in this type of composition, particularly if you use plenty of their leaves and introduce delicate buds towards the top of the oval.

Once it is firmly in place, this main and central stem is complemented by two considerably shorter stems placed one to each side of it. They should be positioned just above the rim of the bowl, tilted forward at an angle of 5° below horizontal. These two stems should be cut to just half the length of the container, plus of course that portion which is hidden from view, as shown in the diagrams.

Now begin to fill in between these stems and the central stem with a mass of flowers and foliage. This is the time to experiment with unusual materials. For example, I love using variegated kale leaves, bunches of parsley and sometimes

Easter, complete with chicken and eggs, even to an egg-shaped oval tablepiece; freesias, ranunculus and roses, placed in a well and held in water in a pinholder, surmount the chocolate eggs

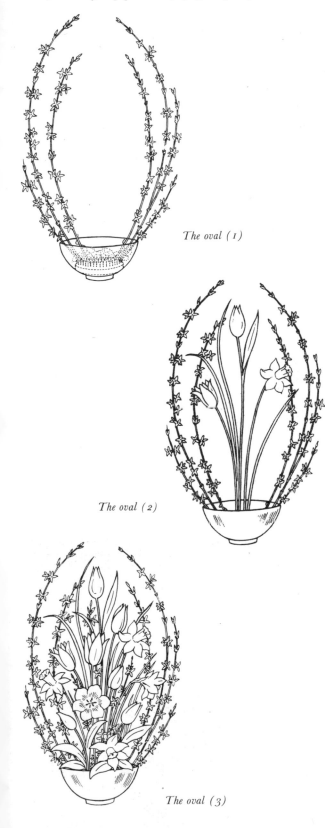

The oval (1)

The oval (2)

The oval (3)

The oval — another interpretation of this design

A rather unusual but most effective variation of the oval is to emphasise a strong line within a mass presentation. This design is particularly well adapted to delicate, flowering, curvaceous shrub branches.

Cut your two main stems twice or even three times the width of the bowl. Place them far back on the pinholder and well to each side of it.

Encourage these two stems to practically meet at the centre top, forming an arch over the container as shown in the diagram.

Fill in by repeating these two lines in varying shorter lengths within the arch. Introduce flowers and materials which are bigger in scale and heavier in texture as you work downwards, also making sure that you are achieving a three-dimensional effect (see diagram).

This type of arrangement is particularly well suited to forsythia viridissima or suspensa sprays, as well as daffodils and tulips.

The perpendicular

The type of container most suited to this arrangement would be a long fruit or salad dish, or a low round bowl. You could also use a Scandinavian wooden cheese or fruit platter as a base, combining it with a small wooden bowl or cream pot in which the arrangement would actually stand, and which should be camouflaged. For a striking, stark effect you could also try a very tall slender piece of pottery, or an unusual wine bottle.

The perpendicular design is symbolic of spring, of the strong upward thrust of young shoots, brave enough to break cover early in the season. It is that upward, surging rhythm which is repeated in the illustrated arrangement of roses and schizostylis. You will notice how few materials are used, and that they are almost entirely upright, very much in contrast to the curves used in previous designs.

Bearing in mind the emphasis on height, cut your main stem more than the minimum $1\frac{1}{2}$ times the length of your container. This must be done to achieve the necessary high narrow look.

Perpendiculars are usually best in flat containers, but exceptions prove the rule. The tall hand-thrown vase is part of the upward sweep of this more unusual perpendicular arrangement. It utilises colourful red dogwood stems, shining green rhododendron leaf bracts and trailing ivy

Impale this stem, leaning very slightly backward, upon the rear of the pinholder, which is of course essential to all flat containers. Since this is a symmetrical design the pinholder should be set well within the centre of the dish. A small piece of wire netting should be firmly embedded on to the pins, but do not let the wire extend over the container, which should be kept absolutely free.

There is no complementary line in this composition — all the flowers and foliage surge upward, following the leader or main stem. Some must be slightly shorter, others considerably shorter. They must all incline at slight angles, the taller ones leaning backwards very slightly, to preserve visual and actual balance. Stems of medium length should be placed more or less upright, whereas shorter stems, placed to the front of the pinholder, should lean forward and sideways leading the eye back to the focal point as well as helping to achieve the proper three-dimensional effect.

Keep the colour and texture light, using 'tight' foliage, and preferably flowers in bud, at the top extremity of the design.

Pink schizostylis and roses with their own foliage soar upward in this hand-made Venetian glass container, emphasising the simple dignity of this perpendicular arrangement

Fill in by introducing depth of colour and solidarity of shape toward the base, but always avoid being too solid in this design. Indeed, if it is early spring when you create this arrangement, copy the Japanese and indicate the season by selecting flower leaves for your main stems with the flowers sheltering beneath, just as they grow at this time of the year (for example, irises and iris leaves).

Check the finished arrangement with an imaginary plumb-line right through the centre. If it is properly balanced, there should be an even weight of colour and form on either side and the top of the arrangement should not be much wider than the focal point (see diagram).

Now cast a critical eye downwards to the pinholder and wire. It is very likely that they are showing, because the delicacy of this fountain-like design makes it nearly impossible to hide these mechanics with greenery or flowers without spoiling the lightness of the composition as a whole. There are, however, two or three quite effective means of concealing them, and you should select the method most suitable to the type of flowers and colours you have chosen. You can use a little moss, placed on the wire and pinholder and allowed to trail off gracefully into the clear water on either side. A few pebbles, banked on the pinholder when irises or primulas were being used, would be very much in unity with these water-loving creatures. A black-and-white colour harmony would be very well set off by pieces of shiny, well-washed coal.

Can you visualise how effective this last colour scheme could be? Imagine an extremely shallow white dish with a shiny black interior. On it is placed a white ramekin dish to hold the water, pinholder and wire, which are concealed by the pieces of coal, and springing upward from this darkness are four or five elegant white gladioli.

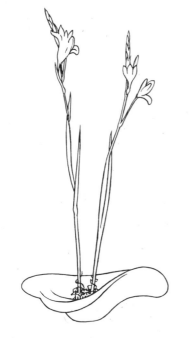

The perpendicular (1)

The perpendicular (2)

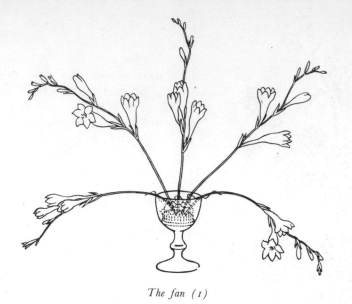

The fan (1)

The fan

This design, with its gentle, soft, rhythmic movement, is the easiest of the symmetrical compositions. Choose for your container a flattish, fan-shaped dish or bowl to suggest the repetitive design. An urn or wineglass is a good choice, as the base is well suited to simulate the handle of a fan.

Use both wire and a pinholder which will fit into the centre base of the vase. If the container is deep enough you could perhaps dispense with the latter, although using both pinholder and wire is the safer measure. Cut your main stem to not less than $1\frac{1}{2}$ times the greatest measurement of your container (plus the usual allowance for unseen stems in the water). Place this first stem in the *dead centre* with a slight backward slope.

Next set the ribs of the fan with an equal number on each side of the main central stem, remembering always to keep your design in correct proportion to the size of your container. Each rib should be cut just a fraction shorter than its neighbour and fixed as close to the central basis as the multiplicity of stems will allow. This ensures there is a very gradual stepping down and angling forward, so that when you finally set the last two ribs in place their position is almost horizontal. They should be tilted forward to $5°$, either below or above the horizontal zero line.

Spiky forms like physostegia, lythrum, larkspur, clarkia or freesias are the best choice for these rib stems. Remember, when you reach the stage of filling in, to maintain the silhouette of these ribs by not placing solid, round flowers directly in front of them. Also, in this case as with all filling in, you should diminish the colour and size of the various materials as they taper toward the outlines.

The fan (2)

14. *Here is an original use for an old teapot! A crescent design of mixed anemones which are held in crumpled wire netting within the pot*

15. *The fan (3). A multicoloured fan arrangement of dainty freesias, a little mimosa and three pale blue irises, held in crumpled wire netting within an opaque pale blue goblet*

16. *The Hogarth curve (3) using cytisus (broom), aucuba foliage and narcissi*

The Hogarth Curve

Eventually an arrangement, however carefully tended, begins to look a bit past its prime. This is sometimes the case after a couple of weeks with winter flowers like chrysanthemums, less with summer flowers, although marigolds will last a month or longer and achillea seem never to die. However, there are still bound to be times when you find yourself faced with a rather droopy-looking arrangement of which some individual flowers or leaves are still bright and cheery. The happiest solution to this problem is to create a Hogarth curve or 'S'-bend.

This is essentially a line arrangement, which means that the emphasis is on good, clean, uncluttered simplicity of line, containing strong movement and no unnecessary fuss or frills. Think of the 'little black dress', simple and unadorned, with all its elegance contained in its beautifully conceived lines. It is a concept which you should keep in mind as you start to create the Hogarth curve.

Your container must be tall, but you should preferably choose one with a shallow water-holder (e.g. a candlecup). You can use a tall, deep container (as shown in the diagram on this page), perhaps a typical old-fashioned vase, but in this case you will require at least two or three very curved stems of flowers or foliage. On the other hand, if the water-holding part of the container is shallow you can angle comparatively straighter, shorter stems, impaling the more perpendicular on the pinholder and knitting the horizontal stems into the wire. In this way you will get the best possible results from this delightful design.

As far as materials are concerned, you need two or three long, nicely curved stems (broom is ideal, but anything else pliable can be used). The remainder of your stems will be cut quite short. Measure your main stem exclusive of its curve. By this means estimate its height in relation to the height of the container. Cut it to measure over the minimum $1\frac{1}{2}$ times in this case, allowing extra for the part which disappears into the vase. Set it far back and secure it firmly with a twist of wire along its stem. The second and complementary stem can now be set in place. It should also possess a good curve, and its measurement must not exceed the height of the vase. Again knit it into position carefully (remember that horizontal lines require very firm fixing), tipping it slightly forward towards yourself. This means that it is curving in the reverse direction to the main stem, which should sway slightly away from you. When this stem is in position you have attained your objective — a delightful S-bend.

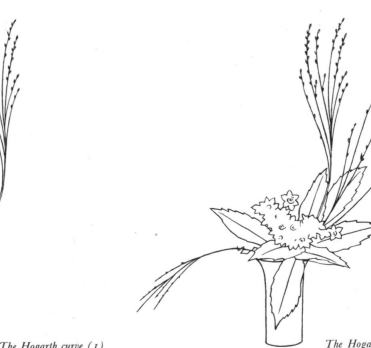

The Hogarth curve (1)

The Hogarth curve (2)

Gracefully simple is this Hogarth curve, consisting of four roses and a couple of trails of ivy arranged within a cone-shaped wall vase, at eye level

Be very careful how you fill in this unusual composition. Remember what I have already told you about Japanese flower arrangement, in which the entire design is based upon a beautiful, uncluttered simplicity of line.

The lazy S-curve must broaden out in the centre, serving the dual purpose of giving depth dimension to the design and effectively concealing the pinholder and wire. You can achieve this broadening by a judicious pen and dart placing of stems and a more acute angling of the very short stems as you descend toward the centre, which is also automatically the focal point and comes into existence without the necessity of being unduly stressed.

Actually, with this type of design it is helpful to practise a slight deviation from the normal filling-in procedure. Once the two complementary stems are in place put a large, opened flower or leaf bract or rosette or cluster of berries or blossoms at the point of focus. Then continue to fill in by tapering upwards and downwards, alternatively following the two initial curves.

Judge your finished picture by looking at it from the sides as well as the front of the design. If it looks interesting and nicely rounded off from whatever angle you view it, then it is successful and you will derive much satisfaction from the arrangement. Incidentally, the Hogarth curve can be varied from the almost perpendicular line to the almost horizontal line to provide a rich wealth of variety.

The crescent

Here is another *pure line* design that is very popular. It is also very useful in between seasons when flowers and long stems are conspicuous by their absence, because its stark simplicity is again economical as far as materials are concerned. All you will need are from two to five semi-curving stems, plus a few attractive short-stemmed odds and ends. Your container can be either flat or of the pedestal type.

If you choose a flat one, let it be either oval or round in shape. A crescent is itself an incomplete circle, and arranging it in a container which is either two-thirds of a circle or a full circle provides a rhythm and repetition of movement which is particularly pleasing to the eye.

If you choose a pedestal container, it could be something like a champagne glass. The flower stems and other mechanics should be attractively hidden by the addition of glass marbles or polished glass chips, when the design is finished. Or you might prefer something like the dolphin vase used in the photograph. In the case of this particular vase, its height is greater than its width. So in order to discover what length your main stem should be, measure the height of the vase. Then cut the main stem $1\frac{1}{2}$ times as long.

The crescent (3)
See colour plate 12, page 53

The crescent (1)

The crescent (2)

Use nature's curves to simulate the new moon. Pink curvaceous antirrhinums and one stem of silver grey senecio greyii establish the crescent outline. Roses and begonias fill in and a regale lily head forms the focal point above the centre rim of this grey and maroon boat-shaped salad dish

The principles of rhythm and repetition are pleasingly obvious in the line of the container and the design of the arrangement

Attach the main stem very firmly through the netting and on to the pinholder. For the placement of this first curving stem visualise the new moon in the sky, and follow the curve through on the opposite side of the pinholder with another, shorter stem, also curving upward. Then, as with the Hogarth curve, decide what material you are going to use for the centrepiece of focal point of your design. If it is a slim, new moon that your crescent is emulating, the centrepiece should be very delicate. If the moon is in its second phase, something larger and heavier will be required, and do not forget to conceal the pinholder and wire netting.

You may then proceed to fill in, using lighter materials and more delicate tints as you taper from the centre towards both ends of the crescent. Use a pen-in, dart-out movement at both the back and front of your design to give depth and relief. Otherwise there is the danger that your crescent will end up so flat that it will look rather as though it has been put through the wringer.

A most pleasing way of using just three pink roses and three buds. My second year-student Miss Irvine has created a crescent with the help of some broom and two pink-flushed Rex begonia leaves, all set in a well-pinholder upon an artistic wooden base

See colour plate 11, page 52

The diagonal

This line at times can look somewhat similar to the Hogarth curve. It can also be rather difficult to achieve if you approach it too casually. The secret is to select your material very carefully, choosing at least one spray or stem that has a graceful fall or bend, as well as a somewhat stiffer branch or spike, which will be used to offset it. Tall containers are usually best, although I have created one diagonal arrangement in a low conch-shell (see page 136). However, height does reveal the line to perhaps the greatest advantage, as can be seen from the arrangement illustrated on this page, which is based on the shape of the container. As this is a jug, or functional container, the upward sweep of the flowers and foliage follows the upward movement of the handle. It then sweeps diagonally down toward and below the lip, emphasising a natural pouring movement.

Diagonal (1)

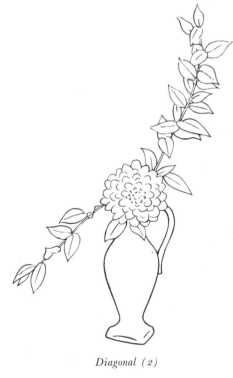

Diagonal (2)

Just an ordinary empty tin, painted and filled with crumpled 2-inch wire netting, holds freesias, begonia leaves and two tulips in another example of the diagonal design

To use this and other such narrow-necked vessels successfully as flower containers, take a very small piece of soft 1½-inch mesh wire netting, and cut to the depth of container, but only about 3 inches wide. Corkscrew this into the jug, leaving some cut ends of the wire standing up beyond the rim. Twist one such end firmly around the handle to anchor the wire netting. The other loose ends can be used to grip and hold firm one or two of the more upright stems, and to help maintain the bend upon the low sweeping material. Since there is not room for many stems, it is advisable to use sprays rather than single heads or, alternatively, compound leaves, which help to fill the arrangement and are economical on stem space. I have used two pieces of golden privet, trimmed to ensure a good uncluttered line. The first stem is cut to twice the height of the jug as seen from the rim upwards, not forgetting to allow for the depth of the container. It should be set at a graceful slope above the handle. The second stem, selected for its in-built curve, is positioned with a downward and slight forward sweep, to complete the diagonal. Both these stems are kept firmly in position by twisting ends of wire netting firmly round their base.

Fill in the design with the cream dahlias and trimmings from the leaf stems. Place the biggest and deepest-coloured flower in the centre with a bit of foliage beneath it to set it off, and let it lean just over the rim, to soften the edge of the container. The second-largest flower is positioned slightly forward and to the left. Two smaller dahlias are placed to lean back in the container,

thus ensuring good balance, both actual and visual. They should also be turned slightly, to make them appear even smaller and less heavy. Do not forget to top up narrow-necked containers with water two or three times a day, to ensure that the shortest stems are always submerged.

All the foregoing arrangements are what are described as frontals. This term means that they are designed to be viewed mainly from the front and sides. Usually they are placed with their

A simple white glazed pitcher, with branches of yew and autumn-tinted ivy set a diagonal line, which emphasises the pouring movement of a jug. 'Up on the handle and down on the spout'. A bract of glossy yellow-spotted aucuba foliage and some bright red skimmia berries complete this colourful and simple arrangement

backs to a wall, or against some furniture, or in a niche at a show. However, it is always wise to tidy the back of the arrangement, just in case it should be seen. After all, it *is* nice to have the back garden as neat in its way as the front of the house. One attractive way of achieving this is to create a miniature arrangement at the rear which is based upon the main design, utilising a few of the discarded bits and pieces. However, you must never let the rear picture superimpose itself on the main arrangement.

Always check the finished arrangement to make sure it is balanced and ascertain that the foundations are not on view. The employment of shells, pebbles, marbles, washed coal and moss all help to conceal the foundations, and to enhance the arrangement if well chosen.

With one exception, soon to be described, frontals are generally worked according to Rule 1. This is the rule relating to the principle of scale and proportion: i.e. that the main and longest stem must be cut to measure at least 1½ times the maximum measurement of the container. It can measure more than this if required, but never less. This height automatically decides the width, and with it the overall dimensions of the whole composition, including both the container and accessories.

Naturally, the shape and type of container you use will also influence the design. Indeed, the container, the design and the size of your arrangement are at all times interdependent.

My second-year pupil Mrs. Turton proves how gracefully the diagonal line can be executed with softly curving foliage like the lonicera and variegated periwinkle which pours downward from the lip of the brightly shining copper jug. Three bright yellow roses repeat the colour at the focal point

The diagonal line can easily become too harsh. Here, it is softened by the elegantly curving larkspur buds and a piece of rosemary. Two delicate gerberas and an ornopordum leaf give it body, and the little accessory completes the movement

A play on the circular design, emphasising the principles of rhythm and repetition. Round frames, in wood or wire, mossed and packed with spray chrysanthemums, Esther Read, scabious and fern, hang above the round table. The pockets of the tablecloth are filled with similar flowers and fern, surmounted by the all-round centrepiece, which combines flowers and fruit

Arrangements placed centrally and viewed from all sides are known as all-round arrangements. The approach to their creation is quite different from that of the purely frontal arrangement, described in the preceding pages. All-round arrangements are created primarily for use on dinner or coffee tables, for private sitting rooms or hotel lounges: in other words, wherever people will be looking at the design from every angle. In such circumstances it is essential no one gets a back view, therefore no back view can exist. As a result, all-round arrangements are a little more difficult to execute than a frontal design, which is created to be seen from the front and sides only.

Although the same basic rules and principles apply, the technical build-up of an all-round arrangement is entirely different from anything we have already practised. And, since exceptions really do prove the rule, you will find that the '1½ times minimum' (Rule 1) will often have to be broken. However, as before, the measurement of the container determines the maximum dimensions of the finished arrangement.

The most valuable and practical variety of all-round arrangement is the kind designed for the normal-sized dinner table. It is the type most often called for in flower shows, and also the most useful one to practise with for home use. For this kind of arrangement the first thing to remember is the size relationship, or principle of scale.

The size and shape of your room have undoubtedly determined the size, shape and perhaps even the period of your table. In the same way the size of your table has a distinct bearing on the type of flower arrangement you design for it. For example, if the room is long and your table is long and narrow, the arrangement would look best and be more practical if it followed an oval all-round sweep. This would ensure that the flowers would not get in the way of the guests sitting on either side of the table, and an oval or oblong container would be the obvious choice. On the other hand, if the table is a large round or rectangle, a somewhat larger all-round arrangement would echo those proportions and a round container would be ideal.

One general point to remember is that you should always avoid heavy strong textures, or very large flowers and foliage for dining tables. The overall effect must be one of daintiness. It is a case of light, lighter, lightest, rather than heavy, heavier, heaviest.

The smaller your table is, the more it will be necessary to ignore Rule 1, regarding cutting the main upright stem to equal at least 1½ times the greatest measurement of the container. This rule must be broken for the simple reason that it is essential that the overall height of the arrangement is low enough to enable conversation to be conducted without everyone having to duck round the flowers. And after all, it is rather nice to see something of your guests! Of course if you are using very delicate, fragile materials like larkspur, brome grass, muscari, freesias or lily of the valley, you may safely use the full height. This also applies if you are using a very small flat container. Otherwise, you should obtain the necessary proportions by extending the 'skirt', a term which I have explained on page 77.

17. *Spring blossom and narcissi combine their ethereal qualities in this delicate all-round dinner-table arrangement. A few coltsfoot and polyanthus leaves, set at base, conceal the pinholder upon which the stems are impaled*

18. *A splash of colour for the mantelpiece, in which the roses and their own foliage, arranged in a simple symmetrical triangle, sweep low over the container*

19. *The finishing touches being given to an oval-shaped all-round arrangement, designed for an oblong table. Roses and spray chrysanthemums are combined with rose foliage*

20. *A horizontal arrangement of grevillea robusta foliage, golden privet and dahlias*

21. *In this design for an oval table all-round arrangement I decided to go gay with a combination of golden privet, sweet peas, roses and buds, ranunculus, phlomis fruticosa and Esther Read chrysanthemums* (Photograph courtesy of 'Woman')

22. *When asked to do this all-round table arrangement I chose a galaxy of summer flowers: nepeta, sweet peas, roses, Esther Read chrysanthemums, phlomis fruticosa, mahonia berries and a little silver-grey cineraria foliage* (Photograph courtesy of 'Woman')

It is essential to get an even all-round effect in an arrangement to be seen from all angles as in this round dinner-table design. Here you see the even, gradual build-up of sweet peas, roses and foliage, forming a slant with the tallest stems of nepeta also in position; all held in a cage surmounting a pinholder (finished arrangement on facing page)

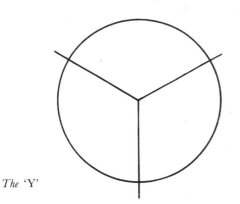

The 'Y'

A circular all-round dinner table arrangement

THE CONTAINER

A round container, either a flat rose bowl or compote dish, on a pedestal is the most appropriate shape for a round table. If the compote dish is slightly taller than its diameter, you should base your measurements and cut your stems according to its height. With a container of another shape (say, of equal diameter, 5 inches, but less height, 4 inches) the diameter would be the determining factor, since it would be the larger measurement.

BUILDING UP THE DESIGN with this type of all-round arrangement is worked by my method of 'skirt' first, then the superstructure, then the 'ears', then filling-in with a slight focal emphasis along the container's rim if required. Such phrases as 'skirt' and 'ears' may sound a little odd, but you will find they play a very important and practical role in the design.

THE SKIRT

Using a paramount holder, or a pinholder covered with a cage, we will start the arrangement with the skirt or outer fringe of flowers or foliage. The stems should be cut to measure either one-third or half the height or diameter, depending on which of these is the larger measurement of your chosen container. They should be placed to look gracefully over the edge of the container,

as if admiring their reflection in the polished table. They should be tilted upwards if a flat bowl is being used, but downwards with a pedestal container, which is the type illustrated.

We will assume that this arrangement is for a round table, and you should therefore work in odd numbers. A round table always has three legs, or three feet to a central column, to give it balance and line, and your design should reflect this fact.

As already stated, your choice should be for the lighter materials such as fern, dainty young spring bracken or the slightly heavier cupressus. This latter, being more strongly textured, provides a more substantial skirt. Or you may prefer small delicate spray chrysanthemums. Whatever your choice, five stems of any of these varieties should be sufficient, and they should be placed equidistant on the outer edge of the circle.

You are now ready to add your second or supplementary skirt. It can consist of either flowers or foliage, depending on which was used for the original outer skirt. It is however, always better to choose different materials for the two layers of skirt. This second circle should have very short stems and should be set further into the bowl, just above the rim of the dish. Your skirt is now completed, and I hope you have made a point of keeping it light and airy.

A red pottery urn, red dahlias (decorative and pompon), eucalyptus leaves and a bunch of parsley combine to make this all-round arrangement a complementary colour scheme with the accent on red

THE SUPERSTRUCTURE

The main stem, to be placed at the centre, should be cut to a maximum length of $1\frac{1}{2}$ times the height of the container (that being the greatest measurement in this case). It must be either a spiky type of stem which faces all ways, such as nepeta, which in flower-garden language is the pretty blue catmint. If however you do not have a stem suitable for this important central position, then choose three slight curving stems of either flowers or foliage. Place them back to back, so that they spring outward as though from an identical stem. In this way you will ensure symmetry of outline from all sides.

You should now moss-up your foundation (the paramount or cage) by inserting extremely short lengths of any suitable feathery greenery. You could also use short stems of flowers such as small bracts of polyanthus, or nigella (love-in-a-mist), which makes an excellent covering with its dainty green Elizabethan collar. Any flowers you use should have their stems cut to about $1\frac{1}{2}$ inches in length.

The reason for this mossing is to make sure your mechanics are completely covered, while still keeping the overall design airy and uncluttered. Proper mossing makes it unnecessary to do a great deal of filling in, with the resultant danger of using too much material, and thus spoiling an otherwise lovely composition just to conceal its foundations. This mossing can also be done for a very wide oval or oblong container, although shapes of this sort do not usually require it, as they are generally fairly narrow in proportion to their length.

THE EARS

The 'ears' are very important as guides and helpers in an all-round arrangement. Their main function is to divide the design into three equal sections to ensure equal distribution of the various materials. Once they are set in place it is advisable to stand up and look down on your design, in order to make sure the ears are really set equally apart. If they are not, then you will probably find that the whole arrangement is a bit lop-sided. As you will discover, it is very easy with an all-round arrangement to find you have used material too lavishly in one spot, and too thinly in another. This is when you will come to bless my system of working with ears, because they are the only safe way of achieving a true balance and symmetry in your design.

The ears may be flowers or foliage, but they must resemble each other as well as being quite different from any other materials you are using. However, they must harmonise in both colour and texture with your arrangement. Once you have chosen your three identical stems, cut them to measure a half or two-thirds the length of the main stem. Place them equidistant from each other in the composition. The angle and height at which they are positioned adds variety to the outline of your composition, but no other flowers or foliage should be allowed to protrude beyond their radius.

Again, I repeat, make sure the ears are of distinctive material. They must be quite different from any other material used in the composition, with the possible exception of the main stem, providing it is a single stem.

An oval arrangement of white bellflowers (campanula barbata), miniature foxgloves, antirrhinums, single stocks, Esther Read chrysanthemums and rosemary foliage are the ingredients of this cool aperitif' for a summer dinner-party

Filling in

A simple method of filling-in, and one which ensures aesthetic balance in your design, is to fill the three 'pockets' between the ears turn and turn about, using an equal distribution of the same types of colours and material. A slightly more difficult, but very charming and unusual method is to use three different types of flowers and three different colour schemes in each of the pockets. This method is particularly useful when you have only a limited amount of any given material. For example, perhaps you have a precious handful of lilies of the valley which would be lost if spread round the whole arrangement. Why not concentrate them in one all-white and cream pocket? The second pocket could contain a delicate mixture of soft blues, including a few precious stems of muscari (grape hyacinth). The third pocket perhaps could be all-pink. Some freesia could be placed here. (Freesia is usually too expensive to use very lavishly.) One word of warning, however; the most important thing in this type of contrasting colour scheme is to provide a link between the three pockets, preferably in both

form and colour. Polyanthus, for example, which can be obtained in blue and cream, as well as a very pretty tone of peach pink, could provide the necessary link. Or you might use identical foliage in each of the pockets, as distinct from any used in the skirt. You can, of course, use the same foliage throughout an arrangement, but whatever your choice, it is most important that the final result gives the effect of being both different and alike.

Continue the filling in by the usual procedure of using lighter, spiky and budded material in light tints for height and deeper tones and stronger forms as you work down to rim level. The rim is the continuous focal point of this type of arrangement and should be stressed with the deepest shades and strongest forms. This intensity of form and colour should taper out to the edge of the outer skirt. It may, if you desire, become as light in tint at that point as the tallest stem or stems. Do not forget to employ the pen-in, dart-out movement, during the process of filling in, in order to give your composition the essential three-dimensional look.

Looking down upon the oval table arrangement showing the exact initial placement of the first stems of the design — the skirt as I call it: (3) and (3) Esther Read chrysanthemums and variegated hosta leaves; (2) and (2) achillea flowers; (1) and (1) curving stems of cytisus foliage. See diagram on page 82

An oval all-round dinner table arrangement

THE CONTAINER

A sturdy, but nevertheless dainty-looking metal container, resembling pewter, is used for this type of arrangement. Let us say that it is to be situated on a refectory table measuring about 7 feet by 2 feet 9 inches. Owing to its long narrow shape it is impracticable to use a pinholder with this type of container, so it should be extremely well wired.

This design is worked from the sides only. Whatever you do, avoid placing anything in the container while looking at it from either of the ends. If you build the sides up correctly you will automatically achieve a balanced and attractive composition at each end. By this method each of the four aspects of your design — two wide, two narrow and elongated — will be equally view-worthy.

THE SKIRT

Begin with the skirt, placing your materials in counts of 1 and 1, 2 and 2, 3 and 3 (see diagram on page 82). This builds both sides simultaneously.

The two shortest stems should visibly measure no more than half the depth of the container, and should hug it and not project.

The second couple of stems are of medium length. They are measured according to the length of the container and should be two-thirds its length, apart from the extra that disappears from view within the container. They should project at an attractive angle, pointing towards the ends rather than to the width, as in the photographs on this page. The third and longest pair of skirt stems are cut to the full length of the container measurement (plus what disappears into the container itself). These are staggered alternately, each fractionally off-centre. Slightly curving stems are best, as their lines both curve away and yet flow back toward the centre, thus achieving a more graceful end elevation. Once these stems have been correctly placed, do not for the moment do any more work on the skirt. Any further necessary material should be added at the filling-in stage, when it can be clearly seen exactly what is needed. By this method you avoid the danger of the skirt becoming too heavy.

Still looking down upon the embryo arrangement, the original placement of materials is supplemented by more Esther Read chrysanthemums, and antirrhinums are introduced before the superstructure, shown on opposite page, above, is placed in position

THE SUPERSTRUCTURE

The superstructure should also be set in counts, 4; 5 and 5, then 6 and 6. Number 4 is the central stem, and is cut to measure either one, or perhaps 1½ times the length of this oval container (allowing extra for the unseen portion of stem in water).

The Number 5's are cut shorter, and placed on either side of the main stem. The 6's (cut shorter again), are placed next, as you can see in the diagrams.

This superstructure, which I call 'rigging the ship', looks its best if the central stem (Number 4) is the only one placed directly central in the container. All the others should be staggered alternately, thus making an interesting depth of design when viewed from each end (see the diagrams page 82). Preferably the central stem should be a spike, rather than a flat flower head. An antirrhinum is most suitable, or perhaps nepeta or lythrum.

Superstructure: consisting of bellflowers (campanula barbata) antirrhinums and single stock

The oval all-round arrangement, nearing completion. Its final effect, when placed on the dinner table, can be seen on page 82

When filling in, follow this staggering of the 'rigging' very carefully. Employ alternately longer and shorter stems, placing the higher, centrally positioned stems with a pen-in movement, and the lower, longitudinal stems with a dart-out movement. This provides the necessary highlights to create the 3-dimensional look. All the points regarding weight and colour at the base, already discussed in this chapter's section on frontal arrangements, apply equally to this design.

The ends of the skirt (stems No. 3), should taper lightly, repeating the quality of the rigging stems, which should be comparatively dainty in form and colour.

The focal point in all-round arrangements lies just above the rim of the container. It may be defined by the use of stronger colour and relatively bolder materials.

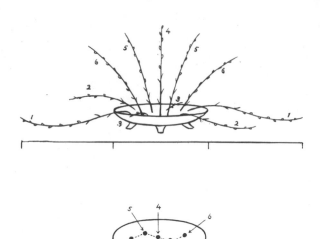

Oval arrangement — correct placing of stems

The oval all-round arrangement, described in the preceding pages, now achieves its place of honour upon the oblong dinner table, for which it was designed. Esther Read chrysanthemums, achillea, roses, stocks, antirrhinums, combine happily with four variegated hosta leaves and a few pieces of broom in a pewter boat-shaped container

A boat of flowers — variation 1 of the oval arrangement

The oval table arrangement - Variation 1

Here is an attractive improvisation of the oval all-round arrangement, particularly suitable for parties. A wicker bread-basket, fitted with a tin lining, holds flowers and foliage so arranged as to follow the sweep of a boat's hull. The rigging, which completes the design, and lifts it by providing scale and proportion, consists of menu cards, shaped to resemble the full-blown sails. For a really luxurious effect you could design one large boat for the centre of the table, with a smaller craft sailing beside each pair of guests. These could bear their names, and a duplicate of the menu.

If a tin lining is not available, substitute Flora-

pak or Oasis, moistened according to instructions, and either cut to fit, or crumpled and packed tightly. The flowers will keep fresh, without the addition of much moisture, for the duration of the party. They can be given a reviving soak later, where there will be no repercussions on the table-cloth!

When placing your flowers, even though you are imitating the lines of a boat, you must keep in mind the basic rules of arrangement. Make sure the flower and foliage stems are placed with a flowing movement from each end toward the centre, which is not in this design otherwise emphasised.

Even a somewhat cramped table must be made to look festive at Christmas. Keeping the arrangement low and flat is one way out of the space difficulty, although this is not an ideal arrangement. However, stately white candles provide the necessary proportionate height in this green and white arrangement which is highlighted by the use of brilliant red skimmia berries nestling amongst the evergreen foliage and their own glossy green leaves

An oval all-round table arrangement - Variation 2

For those of you who prefer a low shallow bowl of flowers on your dining table, here is another version of an oval all-rounder (see colour plate 21, page 75). Proportion is obtained by extending the sideways sweep of flowers and foliage well beyond the side ends of the container. Repeating the upward sweep of this boat-shaped salad dish, the upward flowing, elongated, sides provide the 'lift' so necessary to any arrangement of flowers if it is not to appear flat and uninteresting. This is why it is so important to choose a container which possesses definite movement in its own lines.

The method of working this design is to first place the two main side stems in position. Then, following the rhythm of the container, place your flowers and foliage so that they emphasise the basic lines. Work both sides simultaneously, as has already been explained. Maintain a gentle slope down towards the centre as you fill in. When your design is completed the centre should be markedly lower than the ends.

Correct measurements for all-round dinner table arrangements

As a guide to enable you to choose the right size of container, bear in mind that the height and skirt width are based directly upon the greatest measurement of the container being used.

ROUND CONTAINERS

Let us say the container is taller than it is wide, say 6 inches high, including a 2-inch water holding area. Its height determines that the minimum overall height of the finished arrangement, including the container, should be 12 inches. On the other hand, supposing you have a round container 4 inches in height and 8 inches in diameter, your finished arrangement, including the container, should have minimum measurements of 12 inches in height and 16 inches in diameter.

OVAL OR OBLONG CONTAINERS

Let us say your container is 5 inches in length by 3 inches in depth, and standing on 1½-inch feet. The finished arrangement, including the container, should measure about 9½ inches in height and from 12 to 15 inches in length.

NOTE: All the above calculations are based upon cutting the main stem to same size as the greatest measurement of the container. However, if your table is a very large one, then it will be able to carry a taller arrangement. In these circumstances, and only in these circumstances, you may increase the height of your main stem to a maximum of one and a half times the greatest measurement of the container.

Long supple sprays of luxurious euphorbia lend themselves perfectly to this gracious horizontal design

The horizontal arrangement

This type of arrangement creates a charming line, evoking a sense of peace and repose. Horizontals, although basically a frontal type of arrangement, are exceptions to the general rule regarding measurements which pertain to most frontals.

Of course the measurements are, as always, based upon the container, which must be of necessity tall and fairly slim. A candlestick or something similar is the ideal choice. For those who might query this, I am going to pose a question. Would any tree or weeping shrub be as graceful without its tall slender trunk?

In a horizontal design the height of the main stem varies between only one-third to three-quarters the total height of the container. In relationship to the main stem the horizontal stems, with their sideways sweep, should be cut from three-quarters to once the height of the container. The shorter the main stems, the shorter the horizontal stems will be.

These fluctuations are necessary if one is to obtain the proper proportions in relation to varying thickness of containers, size of base spread, and types and textures of materials. For example,

a rather heavy-looking container such as a somewhat thick turned-wooden candlestick with a three-tier base should be combined with materials like roses and their own foliage, plus other foliage, such as variegated vitis, or some variegated ivy. Such materials, combined with a container like the one described, would follow the lesser ratio proportions. On the other hand, dainty sweet peas, with perhaps some defoliated racemes of Portuguese laurel and cineraria foliage, placed in a silver candlestick, would require the maximum measurements. Also, you should always beware of using very strong, heavy-textured materials, as in a horizontal design, they are not at all suitable for this essentially delicate type of arrangement.

In the horizontal arrangement I am now going to describe, a china candlestick is used. A candle-cup holder is fixed firmly inside it by means of Tide or Selastik. A tiny 1-inch pinholder is also required, plus wire. The materials are a mixture of roses, pinks, curving stems of graceful nepeta (catmint) dainty gladioli nanus (the dwarf variety of gladioli), hosta, saxifraga and mahonia bealei.

Horizontal design (3). Three picture roses, megasea and variegated hosta leaves mark the focal point, with mahonia bealei foliage and flowering spikes of nepeta forming the outline

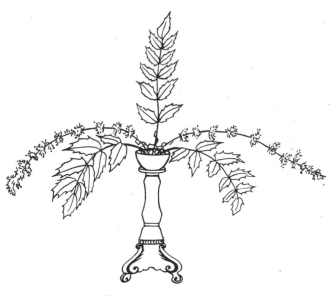

Horizontal design (1)

The outline is set by cutting some sprigs of nepeta and leaf stems of mahonia bealei. These should measure half the length of the candlestick. Place them through the wire and impale them on the pinholder, just off-centre. This is necessary to avoid a too-regular look. Another stem of the same or other material is now cut and should be only the merest bit shorter. It is placed close to the initial stem but should lean slightly more off-centre.

Now choose your horizontal side lines from some young and pliable mahonia bealei. They should be cut to measure two-thirds the height of the container, and are 'knitted' into the wire at an angle of some 5° to 25° below horizontal. The fifth rule, embracing your container, is most essential here, in order to avoid the appearance of a signpost. You must therefore take extra care in setting these stems at the back of the container, making sure they achieve a forward and downward flowing movement (see diagram 1).

Horizontal design (2)

Another arrangement by my pupil Mrs. Turton — her elegant vase-container is made of alabaster, and is perfectly in harmony with the delightful pink roses, pentstemon and laurustinus flowers. A little variegated ivy establishes the downward sweep of the arms of this horizontal design, which maintains its proportion not from the height of the arrangement but from the strongly emphasised sideways sweep

Place one or two stems, a piece of dwarf gladioli and nepeta to the rear of the design and on either side of the two more or less upright central stems. The design is now established and filling in commences.

You should fill in from the centre, using attractive small hosta and saxifrage leaves. Place them so they flow down and conceal the front end of the candlecup container, and soften the line of the candlestick.

Rose foliage helps to cover the foundations and also to make a background for the three roses which combine to form both focal point and a repetition of the over-all horizontal design (see diagram 2, page 87).

A few curving cineraria leaves are placed into the wire in such a position that they curve around the bowl of the candlecup waterholder at both sides and back. The movement is much the same as that of your hands, caressing a brandy glass while you inhale the aroma, or warming themselves around a teacup in very cold weather.

Continue the process of filling in with two dwarf gladioli placed to follow the lines of the nepeta, and tapering to a delicate finish. Short 2- to 4-inch length stems of nepeta are used with a dart-out movement here and there throughout the design, to increase the visual depth, and achieve the important three dimensional look. All colours should be deeper in the centre and fade out to more delicate tints at the side.

Turn the arrangement around and check that the back is neat and tidy, with no ugly wire ends showing. If possible, without intruding upon the design as viewed from the front, create a small repetition of the same picture at the rear. This is really quite a necessary precaution in this type of arrangement, it is low and therefore will be seen most often from above. As a result, any defects of workmanship will be only too apparent.

The summer garden brought indoors — elaeagnus foliage reversed to show the gold and yellow gladioli set the outline. Bright yellow achillea flowers and orange-flushed alstroemeria fill in the centre against a background of large evergreen leaves. A touch of complementary lilac is introduced by the acanthus spikes forming the skirt of this pedestal arrangement

The pedestal arrangement

In this type of design the flowers should look as if they are growing from the top of the pedestal (see colour plate 21, page 93), rather than being 'an arrangement to be placed upon a pedestal' (see picture, page 90). This latter phrase is self-explanatory and is NOT what is meant by the expression 'pedestal arrangement'. A pedestal arrangement is literally one with its stand, and cannot be separated from it or adapted to a different type of base.

Measurements for this type of arrangement are rather difficult to define. To do justice to this most showy and rewarding of all big arrangements you require both experience and practice. But the end results are well worth the effort. Pedestal arrangements are particularly good for parties, especially cocktail parties, where everyone is standing, thus not only endangering smaller table arrangements but invariably rendering them unseen. A good pedestal arrangement, set high at one end of the room, or in the corner of a large room, will command a great deal of attention and give much pleasure to your guests with very little likelihood of accident.

An arrangement on a pedestal — as distinct from a pedestal arrangement. Pale pink tulips, pink megasea saxifrage flowers and trailing freesias suggest the curving lines of this delicate pink natural conch shell

Pedestals vary greatly in design and are not cheap. However, because they are such an intrinsic part of the whole composition, great care should be taken with their selection. Make sure you choose a pedestal that really fits the particular room in which you want to use it. It must harmonise with your furniture and colour scheme. For example, well-polished wood is the best choice for a period room or to complement old-fashioned furniture. Wrought iron, painted in either black or light colours, is more suitable to modern décor. But whatever type you choose, make sure it is stable.

The aesthetic value of the container is unimportant. You do not want to reveal it, rather the reverse, but it must possess certain practical features. It should be flat-bottomed, so that it will hold a large pinholder or paramount holder. As far as size is concerned it should be about 4 inches deep and at least 10 inches in diameter. In other words, it must be shallow enough to allow for a waterfall flow of stems over its sides, but deep enough to contain enough water for many stems, as well as providing plenty of room for them to breathe, and for the free movement of oxygen.

I generally use a sturdy round bulb bowl, colouring the outside to match my pedestal. Being made of earthenware this type of bowl is porous, and therefore the flowers enjoy a relatively longer life. A large, heavy type of pinholder is inserted between the two layers of a paramount holder, and by cutting away one section of the base of the paramount you provide a sufficiently secure foundation for such a large heavy arrangement. A little crumpled 2-inch mesh wire netting is fixed to the paramount. You will notice I say 2-inch mesh, and not the more usual 1½ inch. This large size is necessary, because a pedestal arrangement is required to accommodate more, and usually thicker stems than any other type of design. Leave the ends of the wire upturned; they are very necessary to help secure long, heavy, upright stems, and to exert gently retaining pressure on the horizontal and forward-flowing materials. If you have only a pinholder and wire netting available, then you should fix them more securely by the use of two strong rubber bands (which match the container in colour). Interlace the bands through each other under the container and bring them up at four equidistant points, looping them over the wire ends. The bands and the wire provide each other with mutual and unobtrusive support.

An asymmetrical design, utilising escallonia branches, dwarf gladioli, silvery cineraria foliage, tulips and arum lilies, in a cream-coloured wrought iron pedestal

Most designs or patterns can be adapted to a pedestal arrangement. The easiest is a fan, and next the asymmetrical triangle. A lazy Hogarth curve or crescent is more unusual, but looks most attractive. However, one thing must be borne in mind: to enable the arrangement to look as if it is growing out of the pedestal, forward and downward flowing lines with curves must be employed, best described as a skirt or waterfall movement. It should be kept close to the container at front and sides, and some pieces of material should caress the bowl, as in the horizontal arrangements described on page 85.

All materials chosen for big arrangements should be heavy and comparatively large, although arrangements naturally vary between types of pedestals, and according to the design and material available. And, as in a horizontal arrangement, the heavier the texture and the deeper the colour of material you use, the greater necessity to keep your measurements to the minimum, and vice versa.

As we began this chapter, let us continue by creating the beautiful asymmetrical triangle (see colour plate opposite). Our materials, which will flow from the marble pedestal, are chosen to harmonise with its subdued colouring. We will use soft-toned, grey-green artichoke leaves to curve around and camouflage the container, allowing some more to flow softly away to the sides. The main stem of hyacinthus candicans is measured against the pedestal, and is cut to two-thirds of this length. It is then set very firmly, impaled on the back of the pinholder, with a slight backward tilt, thus ensuring good balance, counteracting the forward pull of later additions and the weight of the skirt flowers. Do not overdo this tilt, however, or the arrangement will look ugly. Two more hyacinthus, cut to slightly different lengths, follow this main stem. We then place three complementary stems; one remaining hyacinthus supported by two stems of lunaria (honesty). The top one is stripped to reveal the shining 'moons' of this attractive plant. The lower stems, in their gorgeous purple and green outdoor coats, are left intact. A twist of wire netting keeps these stems in position.

Seven stately gladioli are now placed so that one becomes the shortest arm of the triangle. The others, moving with rhythmic steps, lend support to the lighter flowers on the perimeter.

Now we turn our attention to the skirt. Using two mauve and one white hydrangea and four regale lilies, we swing the skirt downwards and outwards to give a panniered effect between the lunaria and artichoke leaf. This hides the container, and links the whole arrangement together. However, we must be careful not to overdo this waterfall movement or the arrangement will begin to look like a lady shedding her petticoat! A subtle concealment, with a hint of the container showing through, is the most effective. For the focal point use the rounded forms of hydrangeas, choosing the more vivid tones and deeper shades for the central position at the apex of the three main lines, and set a silver and magenta-coloured begonia leaf among them to provide further accent.

These large flowers and their foliage quite effectively conceal the mechanics of the arrangement. No wire netting is now visible, and two more hydrangeas, white and mauve respectively, are set beside and below the begonia leaf. Thus, a circular rhythmic movement emphasised in colour is set in motion, swinging round and through the whole design, giving us a circle inside an asymmetrical triangle.

Fill in the whole design with many more gladioli, utilising the full-blown stems and deeper intense colour towards the central focal point.

It is especially important that the majority of the stems in pedestal arrangements flow outwards. You will find that handling and placing stems in position with a dart-out movement will assist enormously (see page 34).

When using more delicate materials these outline stems may be increased in measurement. A lot depends, of course, upon the girth and particularly the height of the pedestal itself with regard to increasing and diminishing the measurements. You must, however, beware of trying to match the height of a very tall pedestal by making your main line too tall. You will only succeed in overpowering the room with the arrangement, unless the room is very large indeed. It is usually better to try another design, with less emphasis on height and which relies on its width for proportion. A horizontal, or a lazy S-curve, or a very gracefully drooping pyramid, are all excellent suggestions.

23. *A half-circle of regale lilies emphasises the focal point of hydrangeas and begonia leaf in this asymmetrical pedestal arrangement. Hyacinthus candicans (galtonia), gladioli and lunaria (honesty) form the outline, with a background of artichoke leaves*

26. *A neutral-coloured, grey Victorian slipper supports five dahlias and their own foliage in a curving line design. A complementary colour scheme in orange-red and green*

When the fire is not required fill that eye-catching position with summer's bounty. A cool brass bucket contains a lavish fireplace arrangement in shades, tints and tones of blue, mauve and pink hydrangeas, mauve-tinted grey and white acanthus spikes, purple liatris spikes and white galtonia, spray chrysanthemums and regale lilies, whose mauve stripes render them particularly harmonious. Choose cool colours for warm days

Special arrangements for specific sites and containers (both frontal and all-round)

Mantelpiece, wall vase and fireplace arrangements are all purely frontal designs, and should be worked out according to the basic rules. The only difference between them and the general run of frontal arrangements lies in the varying length of the main stem and the forward-downward flow of material, namely the skirt.

MANTELPIECES

Since these are placed high and are therefore generally viewed from beneath, at least when people are sitting down, they give an elongated view of the main stem. It should therefore be cut to the bare minimum (1½ times its container measurement, see Rule I, page 35). The skirt, since it will be viewed from below, also requires to be exaggerated. It may or may not actually conceal the container. If the mantelpiece is rather low, then the main stem should be extended a little, and the skirt should be proportionately reduced.

WALL VASES

These are excellent for use in crowded rooms where there is no table space to accommodate flowers. Rules governing arrangements for them are similar to those for mantelpieces. However,

they do present a few added problems, because they are generally unsuitable for use with a pin-holder, which means one must rely upon wire netting plus a more than average supply of curvaceous stems. They are nevertheless worth using, as the finished design can look most attractive.

FIREPLACE ARRANGEMENTS

Since this type of design is usually looked at from above, it always presents a foreshortened view of itself. Consequently the main stem should be proportionally much taller than in other arrangements. The skirt for the same reason is practically non-existent.

FLOOR LEVEL ALL-ROUND ARRANGEMENTS

These are generally intended for a central position in the foyer of a hotel or other public places. They are very large, and are worked exactly as an all-round dinner table design. However, the measurements should be considerably 'pulled' or extended, particularly with regard to the height of the main stem. Also the ears can be five, instead of the usual three, although this is not essential.

V COLOUR – HOW IT WORKS

Proportion and colour harmony are the basic essentials of flower arrangement

As we have already discovered, the complementary relationships of the structural parts of a design produce scale and proportion. By the same token, the complementary relationships of differing tints and hues of colour complete the harmony of your picture.

Even if we chose to, we could not avoid using colour in our floral pictures. Even an all-green foliage arrangement is a colour picture, direct from nature's own paintbox, and provides a profusion of hues, with their varying tints and tones.

Emphasising colour, or colours, in your arrangement, is the equivalent of decorating a house once it has been successfully designed. A well-executed arrangement can be much enhanced by the clever use of colour. Similarly, an arrangement somewhat lacking in design and scale can be saved by an arranger who is blessed with a very strongly developed colour sense, or a sound understanding and knowledge of colour.

Conversely, where not enough consideration has been given to colour or where lack of knowledge limits its use, even the best of designs will suffer. However well it is executed, as far as proportion, scale, form-balance and all the other principles are concerned, it cannot reach true perfection if it lacks colour balance.

I have seen a nearly perfect arrangement, good in every other respect, marred by wrong use of colour. An arrangement can be thrown completely off-balance by the introduction of a deep shade of contrasting hue, if it is used in such a manner as to give the arrangement an uneasy, unstable look.

Keeping these important general points in mind, let us try to understand a little more about colour. Let us discuss first of all what it is, secondly how it works, and thirdly, how it can be most effectively used in the art of flower arranging.

Colour is light

In darkness there is no colour. But in the muted tones of beautiful stonework, in dappled sunlight on a cornfield, and in the gaiety of a summer garden, colour is an intrinsic part of beauty.

In 1666, Sir Isaac Newton discovered the spectrum — those wavelengths of light to which our eyes are sensitive. Allowing a shaft of light to shine through a glass prism, and then reflecting it on to a sheet of white paper, he produced a band of colour. (You can do it yourself with the broken edge of a prismatic-patterned glass.) It is, in fact, an exact replica of a rainbow. Unshed raindrops in the atmosphere act as the prism for a beam of sunlight which is colourfully reflected in the sky.

If we look at the rainbow of colours on our own privately produced replica, we see it consists of seven main hues: *Violet, indigo, blue, green, yellow, orange* and *red*. Although indigo was included by Newton, and is very definitely seen in the spectrum, for some reason it gets left out when the spectrum colours are mentioned, so they are often listed as merely six in all.

Skilful colour harmony creating a play on design emphasised by colour. Gunmetal-coloured canna and yucca foliage combine with brilliant red mahonia bealei leaves to frame the cream chrysanthemum and stocks

An arrangement which cannot be faulted: three bronze chrysanthemums attended by yellow dahlias, some flushed with pink, others a delicate apricot, follow a majestic upward sweep in this beautifully executed asymmetrical triangle. The golden beech leaves form a subtle depth of undertone and a link between the natural wood base and these simple flowers. My fourth-year student Mrs. Hunt has proved that she has thoroughly assimilated the art of arranging flowers

Between the chemists who make our artificial or pigment colours and the physicists who study colour derived from sunlight (natural light) opinion differs as to whether there are three or four primary colours. Chemists subscribe to only three, but physicists, backed by physiologists, maintain that there are four primaries. These are red and green, blue and yellow. This theory is based upon the fact that the human eye responds to these colours simultaneously, as will be explained later in this chapter.

The language of colour

The word *Colour* is a general term, embracing all colours. Therefore when we want to be more specific, we must talk of *Hues, Tints, Shades, Tones* and *Values*.

HUE: This is a *Pure* colour, with no addition of black or white.

TINT: This is a *Lightening* of the pure, or basic hue by the addition of white.

SHADE: This is a *Deepening* of the pure hue, by the addition of black.

TONE: This is a *Chromatic change* of the pure hue, by the addition of an admixture of black and white, which is of course grey.

VALUE: This describes the *Colour intensity* of the hue.

In case you find these five definitions a little confusing, I will give you a tip. My own method of remembering them is to think of the pure basic hue as seen in the spectrum as the 'waistline'. Above the waist are the tints and below the waist are the shades. But do remember to be tactful with your new knowledge. If you hear a friend talking about wanting a lighter shade for her drawing-room curtains, you will now realise that what she actually means is a lighter tint. You must find a gentle way of explaining to her that talking about lighter shades is tantamount to saying 'going upstairs-down'.

When we are dealing with nature's bounty of flowers and foliage, we find our colours supplied in such infinite variety that caution becomes the watchword. It becomes a case of 'How much can I leave out?' rather than 'How much can I use?' This is why a great deal of thought should go into planning a colour scheme even for a simple flower arrangement.

Colour - how it works

You may be wondering how all this talk of the rainbow and the spectrum can help in arranging flowers. I will try to explain. First, imagine the rainbow as a complete circle with red and violet merging into each other. You have now created in your imagination the mystical colour circle you may sometimes have heard people mention. If you look at the inside back flap of the dust jacket of this book you will see a colour circle which you will find very useful for reference. You can even cut it out and hang it up in a convenient place.

The central band of our circle represents the true hues of the spectrum. The outer circle, with the addition of some white, portrays the tints. The inner circle, with the addition of some black, gives us the shades. You will notice I have broken the circle into groups of three. The central hue is flanked on either side by tones, all with their relative tints and shades.

An all-green arrangement is refreshing in summer as a contrast to the galaxy of colour in the garden. Here rosettes of daphniphyllum are used instead of flowers. The shiny lighter green ligustrum and mahonia japonica foliage complete the drooping pyramid design

Colour schemes

ANALOGOUS

Neighbouring colours are in harmony with each other because they have a common denominator. For example, blue and violet both contain blue, red and orange both contain red. In the language of flower arrangement using up to three, but preferably only two neighbouring colours, is known as an *analogous* scheme. An arrangement in tints, shades and tones of blue, mauve and maybe green is a good example of this type of colour scheme.

MONOTONE

The use of one hue only, but utilising the full gamut of all its subtle tints, shades and tones, is a *monotone* scheme. For example, suppose yellow is chosen as the basic hue, the variation in colour can range from a rich shade of ochre to the palest lemon yellow.

COMPLEMENTARY

The use of two colours directly opposite each other on the colour circle, plus their respective tints, shades and tones creates a *complementary* harmony. It is often used by nature herself, as in a dark red peony and its green leaves, or the touch of strong yellow on the petals of a blue iris. The one colour plays off the other, so to speak, intensifying our pleasure in both.

THE PHYSICAL EFFECT OF COLOUR

According to medical opinion, the human eye accepts the four primary colours in pairs. The rod and cones of the retina of your eye see red/green and blue/yellow simultaneously (a balance of one warm and one cold hue).

To prove this interesting fact for yourselves, try the following experiment. Stare at a piece of green material (the bright green cardigan of a friend, for instance) for thirty seconds. Then immediately transfer your gaze to a blank neutral grey- or white-coloured wall. You will now see a red cardigan, and vice versa. The same thing happens with blue and its complementary colour, yellow.

These are known as after-images. This knowledge helps when arranging flowers, or choosing a background for them, because the complementary colour enhances its mate. The red flower looks a deeper and richer red, because the after-image from the green leaf makes you see red. However, for the best results, make certain that one of the complementary colours is more emphasised than the other.

This same phenomenon of the after-image is also effective in combinations of white or grey, when used with a pure hue. Some of the complementary hues will be reflected in the neutral shade. For example, white would look yellow used with blue. Thus a blue and white flower arrangement would, in fact, look more colourful than it sounds.

After-images are seen by all who are not colour blind, and it is interesting to note that colour blindness occurs in pairs of the light primaries. Blindness to red-green is more common than the inability to see blue/yellow. This affliction occurs more often in men than women!

TRIADS

Three colours, spaced equidistant on the colour circle, and being neither neighbouring (analogous) nor purely complementary, are known as *Triads* schemes. They are not ideal for arrangement, as they do little to help each other in creating a harmonious colour scheme.

POLYCHROMATIC

Where four or more colours are used together, you have a *Polychromatic* scheme. Again, not ideal for the flower arranger, except when doing a very large design, when each hue can have a free range. Colours should be tinted out to become almost white for the highlights, and shaded to almost black for the depth, where the hues merge into each other. Both triad and polychromatic schemes may be used for interpretative arrangements to express a particular idea or theme. For example, suppose you are using the figurine of a flower vendor and your arrangement is to represent all the various bouquets he has for sale. Even under these circumstances one has to be very careful, in grouping the colours, to make the arrangement effective.

Do not imagine that if you limit your colour combinations to one or two hues, or at the most, three, your arrangements will be dull. Considerable variation can be achieved by using the many values (tints, tones and shades) of the chosen hues, producing a most colourful harmony. And it *will* be harmony, not discord! To give an example, suppose we take orange and then incorporate three or four or more of its values, ranging from a soft dull shade of brick for the container to the palest peach-pink flowers and buds. Split-complementary accent can be provided by various values of green.

Grey is a neutral, and can be used to introduce variety within a given colour scheme. It mixes happily with either the warm colours of the spectrum (the reds, oranges, yellows), or the cool colours (the blues, violets and greens).

If you analyse arrangements which employ the usual toned green foliage, you will find they are semi-analogous, with a touch of complementary provided by the mate of the dominant hue. For example, a yellow pottery bowl of marigolds, in their pure hues of orange and deep yellow combined with their own foliage, are marvellously set off by a few trails of tradescantia, v. tricolor, a creamy yellow leaf with definite violet and pinky-mauve markings.

The psychological effect of colour

Having dealt with the physical effect of colour on ourselves, we now come to an aspect which is even more important to the flower arranger — that of the emotional responses colour sets up in us: its psychological effect.

Light and heat both come from the sun, and within this light are colours which can be either warm or cool, exciting or depressing.

The warm hues are those nearest to the sun colour as we see it. They are red, orange and yellow, and the effect they have on us, through their visual impact, is to convey warmth, and a feeling of goodwill and cheer, even of excitement. But also, on the other side of the scale, red suggests anger and all such strong emotions, so much so that we have evolved sayings like 'red-hot anger' and 'painting the town red'.

Violet, blue and green are the cool hues, because the visual impact they have on our senses is one of coolness and quiet. They promote a feeling of peace and tranquillity, but they can also cause one to feel depressed and even morbid. The saying 'a fit of the blues' expresses this very vividly.

The truth of the matter is that all the pure hues are so intense that we instinctively keep clear of them in large doses. We prefer to surround ourselves with a judicious mixture of tints and shades of both cool and warm colours. The mixture we choose depends on ourselves, our own colouring, our particular nature. Excitable people, prone to nerves, are happiest when surrounded by the cool blues, mauves and greens which act on them as a sedative. This also makes these colours more suitable for bedrooms. On the other hand, calm, placid people require the stimulus of the warm oranges, reds and yellows—certainly yellow is an antidote to depression. But as you can now see, it is all interrelated: colour disposition, and the effect colours have upon us.

Roses, chrysanthemums, rhododendrons, carnations and stock create a delightful splash of mauve-pink colour, arranged on a pinholder and cage inside the burnished copper saucepan

Colour and temperature

Having discussed how colour reacts upon us physically and emotionally, we are now ready to consider it in another aspect — the relationship between colour and temperature.

It is a well known fact that white and tints (those colours to which white has been added in varying degrees) reflect the sun's rays, and therefore are heat resistant. That is why people in the tropics paint their houses cream, or, better still, white, and wear mainly white and pastel-tinted clothes. By doing this they are warding off much of the sun's heat. My great uncle, a general in the veterinary corps in India, told me that grey horses were much sought after for the cavalry. It seems they were less prone to suffer from heat than the more usual bays! Tints are cooling, especially tints of the basically cold hues.

Black and shades (hues with black added in varying degrees) absorb the sun's heat. Therefore if we wear deep shades, and use them to decorate our houses, we help to keep ourselves and our surroundings warmer. It is not by accident that our designers produce winter clothes in warm dark colours for our northern hemisphere. And we have all read some descriptive passage about walking by a sun-warmed mellow brick wall, which conjures up an immediate vision of a hot summer's day. (Unfortunately we always seem to read such sentences in midwinter!) You will notice the colour of the bricks was mellow, therefore they are dark rather than white. A white wall would indeed have made the passers-by warmer than the brick wall, because it would have reflected the heat on to them, although the visual reaction would have been cool, whereas the brick wall would be greedily absorbing all the sun's heat, and passing it through

to the house behind. Shades, we have discovered, are warming, especially the shades of the basically warm vibrant hues. Black and white are recognised as colours, because they have a visual and symbolic reaction upon us. Black is warm, because it has a maximum heat absorption, and since it is the final repository of all shades it reflects no light. White is cool, because of its maximum heat and light reflection. There is a link here, too with its claim to represent purity.

'Very interesting', you may be saying, 'but I still don't really see where flower arranging comes into all this.' Or have you, perhaps, begun to guess?

As we have already said, flower arranging is a creative art and should therefore reflect your personality. But your arrangements should also be created for the benefit and joy of others. Supposing you have invited some guests to lunch on a scorching summer day and they leave after barely touching your carefully prepared food. You are naturally upset. Have you stopped to consider that the rich warm shades of red and brown with which your dining-room was decorated could have had something to do with your guests' lack of interest in the food? And the beautiful matching flower arrangement, repeating the strong reds and yellows and sitting in its red container in the middle of the dining-room table, might well have been the last straw for heat-reduced appetites.

On the other hand, supposing it is a wet, bitter winter afternoon. In your drawing room, which faces north, you have placed a lovely analogous arrangement in soft lilacs and greens. Are you really surprised that the friends who drop in for tea noticeably fail to appreciate it?

Again, you are visiting a sick friend in hospital. He is recovering from a stroke, and you most thoughtfully plan to take him a little flower arrangement, to place by his bedside. You are a tranquil soul and adore the brightening and exhilarating effect of gay flowers. Remember to be cautious. Orange-red and yellow are the 'heating' colours and you would not want to send your friend's temperature soaring again. A much wiser choice would be a simple arrangement, executed in varying, soothing shades of green. On the other hand a young convalescent mother, in the grip of post-natal blues, would love a brightly coloured arrangement and it would be just the thing to cheer her up.

From such examples as these you can see just how important a function colour plays in our lives, acting not only through our visual sensations but in relation to temperature as well.

We flower arrangers are working in full colour all the time. Therefore it is most important that you do spend a little time studying the colour circle. It is not necessary for you to run round the garden with your flower scissors in one hand, and the colour-circle chart in the other. But you should become familiar with the tints and shades which are related to any given basic hue, as well as knowing those which are neighbours (analogous) and those which are complementary. You should also begin to appreciate the great range of colour that can legitimately be worked into a scheme which consists of one basic hue (monotone). And finally, you should also become aware of the extremely useful functions of the neutral grey.

On the inside back flap of the dust jacket underneath the colour circle is a colour strip which illustrates one of the tints and shades of pink — the mauve-pink. There are two separate pinks, no matter how delicate the final colour. The first, which is illustrated, has its roots in magenta red, the second in orange red, which shades down to orange-pink, and is commonly called peach.

With very few exceptions, we all experience colour sensation. Generally, however, we lack awareness of the considerable influence of colour upon us and our surroundings. Increased knowledge and understanding of language of colour is a way in which our subconscious awareness may be brought to the surface of our conscious minds. Gradually, you begin to perceive colour consciously and to understand it by analysing its effect on yourself and others. It was with this purpose in mind that the present chapter was written, not only to help you use colour more effectively, but also to increase your enjoyment of it.

How to employ colour in flower arranging

Whatever design you plan, be it a horizontal, an asymmetrical triangle, a fan, etc., always apply the shades in their greatest intensity low down in your arrangement. A deeper-coloured flower is visually the heavier flower, therefore keep it down towards the base, and very much into the hub or focal point of your arrangement, so as to 'anchor' it.

Set the vertical outlines with the lightest tint in the highest position. This, incidentally, is the ideal position for buds, but be careful you do not choose a bud (perhaps a rosebud) which is destined to burst into a deep coloured flower. Make certain it is the bud of a flower which is light in

As is so often the case when a man steps into the province usually occupied by mere woman, Mr. Chapman reveals himself as a second-year student of distinction! Here he arranges golden beech leaves and pale yellow chrysanthemums in an asymmetrical triangle. The flowers and foliage are held on a pinholder inside a shallow elongated container. Three bronze dahlias repeat the rhythm of the design and mark the focal point

The colour-weight of dark green Portuguese laurel leaves set so high throws this arrangement of spray chrysanthemums out-of-balance, rendering it top heavy

colouring. Horizontal extremities, on the other hand, can afford to be a trifle deeper in tone. Thus you work from the outer edges, blending the colour values gradually inwards toward the deepest shade at the base and, through this correct placement of colour, you will always achieve colour-balance. Even if your design as a whole is not too well balanced, you can pull it together and correct its deficiencies by placing the extra colour-weight where it is required.

COLOUR-BALANCE — HOW IT CAN GO WRONG

Let us say you are working with some tall, daintily proportioned flowers, such as the old-fashioned Grannie's bonnet aquilegia in a plum shade, plus a variety of roses. You will soon find yourself in a quandary. If you set the aquilegia high and the heavier-looking but lighter-coloured roses low, you will not be pleased with the results. The eye will be drawn to the aquilegia because of their colour strength, and the arrangement will give the impression of being top heavy. In other words, the colour-balance will be incorrect.

FORM-BALANCE — HOW IT CAN GO WRONG

It is equally obvious that if the aquilegia is cut short and placed at the focal point it still will not look right, in spite of its colour. The larger and heavier-textured roses (although lighter in tone) will outweigh the aquilegia. Again the balance will be thrown out, in this case the form balance.

COLOUR AND FORM-BALANCE — TO SYNCHRONISE

A means of correcting both the above problems is to first place a rose, shaded as deeply as the aquilegia, at the focal point of your design. Then put a smaller rose, not quite such a dark one, close to it but a bit further up. Continue to follow the main upward movement of your design with the dark-coloured, delicate aquilegia. If, however, you have no deeper shades among the roses, you must use a bract of copper beech, or any flower or foliage which gives colour depth, to provide the aquilegia with a substantial foundation. By this means you avoid allowing its strength of colour to dominate the design.

Remove those leaves and the colour-balance is restored and form-balance in the design is improved; set well within the handle of the trug basket

Always avoid splashing colours about indiscriminately in an arrangement. It creates a feeling of restlessness and disharmony. Group your colours, especially if using many hues with their varying tints and shades and intensity of values, as in a polychromatic scheme. And in this latter case make good use of neutral grey to help blend your various colour groups.

USE COLOUR TO EMPHASISE DESIGN

If it is an asymmetrical triangle you are creating, apply the principle of repetition by repeating that design with three well-chosen deep-shaded flowers placed triangularly at the focal point. Or you could use a triangular cluster of brilliantly coloured berries, or bracts of rich-textured, very dark foliage in an all-foliage arrangement (e.g. daphniphyllum). If it is a fan-shaped or another type of symmetrical arrangement, the colour accent could again emphasise that line. For example, a Hogarth curve would look particularly lovely if a strong sweep of deep colour, graded in shade and intensity (and of course in size), swung from the top of the S-curve to the bottom.

YOUR CONTAINER MUST ALSO BE INCLUDED IN YOUR COLOUR SCHEME

In fact, it should be treated as the senior partner, with the exception of pedestal and mantelpiece arrangements, where it is hardly seen. Most effective results can be obtained if it tones with the highlights and tints of the lightest values in your colour scheme, thus sandwiching the deep colour in the centre of the design. For example, try using a pale peach-pink container in conjunction with deep-shaded salmon, apricot and peach-pink flowers, and natural bronze foliage (a monotone scheme). However, the container must be strong enough, in both texture and form, to cope with the form and colour of the arrangement it holds. Otherwise you run the danger of your design looking as though it is floundering in mid-air, without visible means of support. If you are attempting a colour scheme such as the one suggested above, and are not sure that a pale pink container would look substantial enough, make the safer choice of a rich cinnamon or salmon pink one.

Your container may also echo the dominant colour in the arrangement. For example, if you are designing an analogous scheme, using blues and pinks and mauves, your container could be blue or mauve. However, it *must not be pink*, because in this colour scheme pink is the outsider, and should serve only as an accent. A pink container would equalise the colours of the entire arrangement, and for a really successful effect one basic hue or colours arising from a common denominator *must be dominant*, if the effect is to be truly harmonious.

This question of a dominant colour is particularly important in flower arranging. As with all good marriages one partner should have the prevailing influence, although each remains important in his own right. Therefore, if you are using a complementary arrangement between mauve and yellow, one or the other of the two colours must be dominant. In this case the master colour is most likely to be yellow, because of the foliage. There is so much yellow in many of nature's tones of green that plenty of choice would be provided for this type of colour scheme. To lend further emphasis your container should also be a shade or tone of yellow.

IN ALL COLOUR SCHEMES, with the obvious exception of the monotone, there must be one hue dominant over all the others. The reason for this is physiological. As we have already learned, the eye sees two colours simultaneously. If one is forced to look too long at a completely equal division of these two the nerves of the eye become strained, and rebel. The result is that one literally begins to see things which are not there.

Spots appear before the eyes, and even splodges of grey at the centre of vision, which spoil one's pleasure in the colours being regarded.

Neutral grey plays a particularly useful part in separating colours that do not harmonise or mix happily. Grey foliage is particularly useful when, if entering a competition, you find yourself faced with a request for a specific colour scheme. For example, if asked to create an all-blue arrangement, you may be quite worried about the best foliage to choose. You can solve the difficulty by utilising the really lovely silver grey foliages, such as cineraria maritimus, senecio greyii, or the grey elaeagnus.

Black containers are also considered as a neutral and are extremely useful. Combined with vibrant colours and textures, the container will act like a good coachman, well in control of his spirited four-in-hand.

White containers are another neutral. They will not obtrude upon the most delicate of pastel arrangements, and look simply lovely when combined with all-white arrangements.

One note of caution. So many vases and pottery bowls are produced in garish sweet-shop colours which are difficult to use successfully. This is particularly true of the so-called greens which often clash violently with naturally coloured leaves and stems.

An analogous scheme is represented by this sheaf of yellow tea roses with their light green foliage, bound with shimmering gold ribbon

VI 'OCCASIONAL' ARRANGEMENTS

For anniversaries, parties, Christmas, churches and weddings

Originality springs from within!

We have now reached the stage where we have learned the basic rules and principles regarding flower arrangement, as well as becoming familiar with the necessary tools and techniques. We have gained knowledge and understanding of the language and use of colour, and have actually carried out a number of arrangements. This

A wrought-iron wine bibber makes an attractive container for tulips, polyanthus, geranium and a begonia leaf, held on a pinholder and wire netting in this graceful diagonal design

chapter also deals mainly with arrangements, but in this case with designs which are created for a special purpose and for a special occasion, such as decorations for churches and Christmas, for weddings, anniversaries and parties.

However, before I begin to describe the arrangements themselves, I would like to spend a little time discussing three very important terms. These are *arrangement*, *composition* and *interpretative arrangement*. An analysis of these terms will be of particular help to those among you who want to exhibit at flower arrangement shows. They will also be of considerable interest and help to beginners, and to those whose showground is their own lovely home.

An arrangement

This phrase sums up all the component parts of your design: *(a)* the natural materials, flowers, buds, foliage, fruit and berries; *(b)* the pinholder and/or wire netting on which they are held; *(c)* The container, and with it perhaps some sort of simple base, which is only allowed if it can be said to 'belong' to the container: for example, a simple wicker mat beneath an earthenware vessel which contains a Japanese style arrangement, or perhaps a wooden base, designed to go with a particular vase. Either of these would be considered an intrinsic part of the whole, rather

than an extra or accessory. Driftwood may also
be included within the actual design.

A composition

As its name implies, this is an arrangement in
which additional non-plant material is used to
render it even more effective. These accessories
may take the form of a drape of some lovely
analogous or complementary material or an
ornament, a figurine, a piece of dinner-service
plate, or even a candle. There can also be a sub-
sidiary arrangement of natural material: anything, in fact, which contributes to the whole, and
provides a bigger and better show. In a flower-
picture such as this, composed with a complete
design in mind, all the components should lead up

to and dramatise the focal point of interest, which
should be within the main part of the composition. Avoid letting an accessory steal the show or
otherwise lead the beholder's eye away from the
design as a whole. Accessories, whatever they may
be, must be subservient to the arrangement, and
by their clever employment should emphasise or
dramatise some particular feature of the natural
plant material. They must be so necessary to the
design that it appears unbalanced or incomplete
without them. Test your design by taking away
the accessory you intend to use. Does the arrangement satisfy you? Is it complete? If it is, then the
accessory is superfluous and it is wiser not to use
it. On the other hand, if you carefully analyse the
whole composition, you may find something else
can be removed, thus allowing the accessory to do
a really effective job. But remember always to
keep it in scale. It is, after all, only an accessory
and the natural plant material must dominate
a composition, particularly when entering a
competition.

Barbecue arrangement

Interpretative arrangements

These go one step further than either arrangements or compositions. They are used mainly for
exhibitions and composition at flower shows. The
main emphasis is laid upon a theme or idea to be
conveyed. This theme is most carefully interpreted by the considered choice of the accessories,
container and background for the natural materials. Indeed, the actual arrangement should take
second place to the clear and vivid presentation
of the theme. In fact, although usually captioned,
the message of an interpretative arrangement
should be self-evident. A judge would actually
have to by-pass a better arrangement if its message was not clear, in favour of a less attractive

arrangement which interpreted its chosen theme
effectively.

A BARBECUE

As I have already said, interpretatives are used
mainly for competitive show work. However, they
can be employed most impressively as party pieces
for one's home, like the barbecue arrangement
featured here, which I created for my own party.
This type of composition is particularly effective
in the hall of the house. It both welcomes
the guests, and indicates the nature of the
party and where it is being held (in this case,
out of doors, in the copse adjoining the house.

The drape of tree-patterned material indicates the copse. The all-round arrangement of bright red geraniums, flame and yellow gladioli nanus, and miniature foxgloves, represent the fire rising from the outdoor brazier. Beneath, lie the burnt logs and red-hot ashes, the last interpreted by red glitter left over from Christmas decorations.

Such a design clearly conveys its message: the nature of the party, plus an admonition to the guests to keep their woollies on and hasten out of doors to join the merrymaking, so delightfully conveyed by the flower arrangement.

A CHEESE AND WINE PARTY

Why not create a composition to decorate the table on which your varieties of cheese are being served? Utilise a cheese dish, plate or board for the base of the arrangement, and combine driftwood, moss and a figurine with some flowers and foliage (see colour plate No. 30, page 115).

A SWEET-SEVENTEEN BIRTHDAY PARTY

A bunch of violets, with their stems loosened from the restraining string or rubber band (and varied as to height) are lashed to a stout piece of woody stem. This is then impaled on a pinholder and set in a pale green goblet (as shown above). A linen cloth, in a complementary colour, is used as the base for the goblet, and this colour contrast is as exciting in its effect on the violets as is the party for the birthday girl!

Violets in a green goblet

31st October — and the witch appears to be brewing a cauldron of mischief! Vivid dahlias, ivy, fruit and 'nameless horrors' combined with the well-arranged drape, are the ingredients of this clever interpretative arrangement

A small posy of flowers arranged with a little suitable foliage makes that gift parcel doubly attractive! One lovely gardenia or camellia held against three of its own leaves. The stems are wired together, placed in slightly damp moss, which is held in position around the stems by a twist of florist's cellophane. The posy is fixed to a dark red-wrapped package by a piece of Sellotape, hidden beneath an attractive cellophane tie.
Two other parcels offer the lucky recipients gorgeous smelling freesias and one perfect rose, offset by simple colourful ivy leaves.
Another sports single carnation and variegated tradescantia trails. These flowers are all chosen for their longlasting qualities and, provided they are conditioned by a good pre-delivery drink and placed in a posy bowl of water immediately on arrival, they will give much additional pleasure.

OTHER PARTY PIECES

Place your arrangements high on mantelpieces, a corner cupboard or a tall shelf, particularly if you are giving a cocktail party, because then they will be seen and not sat on! A tall pedestal arrangement also commands attention without getting in the way, if it is placed in a far corner. Nevertheless, one small arrangement can be fun and very effective too, particularly if placed on the table where the drinks are being served. Try

linking the flowers and the wine, as in the arrangement shown on page 35. It consists of left-overs from a larger composition, using only three phormium leaves, a couple of bright-eyed red anemones and a bract of evergreen. Make sure that the stems reach well down into the bottle, and top it up with water at least twice a day. There is no need for any wire netting; in fact, there will be no room for it. To hold the stems in position, insert the main stem first. Then, holding it firmly with the finger of one hand, introduce the other stems in turn. Hold each new stem back against the side of the bottle with yet another finger, and place the last flower and bract of foliage so as to conceal the rim of the bottle. Alternatively, place the main stem, cut to the necessary proportions first, and then arrange the other stems in the palm of your left hand, before easing them into position all in one piece. Equally effective is the empty liqueur bottle shown on this page, in which begonia flowers and some briony spray, combined with a dried ivy branch, form a line arrangement. This is particularly suitable to place by the canapés and other delicacies accompanying the drinks you serve.

27. *Yellow daffodils combined with their own foliage, some iris leaves, muscari and a trail of ivy, placed in a neutral grey stone bowl. This is basically an analogous colour scheme, but the introduction of the white ducks and stones transforms it into a more colourful composition*

28. *A green and white composition of chrysanthemums arranged in an antique bronze inkwell. The ornamental top of the inkwell is used as an accessory to balance the design*

29. *A hamper basket of mauve-pink, shot with gold, holds pale, mauve-pink spray chrysanthemums, and four deeper-shaded disbudded chrysanthemums. This is a monochromatic or one-colour arrangement. The preserved eucalyptus foliage, although mainly a neutral soft grey, also contains touches of mauve*

30. *A composition employing the principle of repetition as expressed by the lines of the bird and the driftwood. The base is a cheese board. The fern is growing upon the moss, and the violets are held in a pinholder concealed beneath the moss*

31. *In this design full advantage is taken of the ornate mantelpiece, so deserving of really grand treatment. (This mantel is in Oldway Mansion, Paignton.) The mahonia bealei leaves, the pale yellow euonymus foliage and the yellow-spotted aucuba, have formed a colourful background for many different flower arrangements during the long winter months. Now bright daffodils and golden forsythia bring the glow of spring to this arrangement of 'evergreens'*

32. *Summer and autumn mingle happily in this sweet-smelling basket of chrysanthemums and freesias, combined with a little shredded pampas grass and foliage*

ANNIVERSARIES

These are occasions of such particular importance that they call for special flower arrangements throughout the house, as well as providing that spark that will fire you to your imaginative best. For example, twenty-five years' happy marriage certainly calls for celebration. There is your husband's gift of dark red roses: why not arrange them on the table with the decanter and glasses to extend a really warm welcome to your guests, as shown in the picture on this page? If, on a cold winter evening, the table is set against a rich red velvet curtain, with the bright firelight leaping at its own reflection in mirror or window panes, the effect of warmth and good cheer will be quite magical. Notice in the photograph of this arrangement how the decanter and glasses are so placed as to lead the eye in to the focal point rose, at the base of this asymmetrical triangle design.

Anniversary roses

A FIRST BIRTHDAY PARTY

If it is the small daughter of the house there should be pink and white icing on the cake, and one pink candle. And on the front door a welcoming circlet or garland, consisting of delicate pink roses and leaves wired to a simple mossed-up frame, surmounted by a large pink ribbon bow, as the picture shows. This sort of arrangement is also suitable for a christening. These rings, already mossed, can be purchased from a florist. You can also buy different shapes, or even knock up a simple wooden frame and moss it yourself. But you will need literally buckets of moss! If you live in the country it is quite easy to obtain fresh moss, but it is amazing how much is required to pack the frame tightly, and it must be firm if it is to be effective, and for easy manipulation. The correct method is to take a handful of moss and press it around the frame, holding it in place with one hand, while you bind it tightly with twine. Then add the next handful, being careful to leave no gaps or thin places as you work.

The leaves and flowers should first be wired with florists' stubs. Fix the wire to the calyx of the rose and twist it down the shortened flower stem. Then secure it to the mossed frame by pressing the end of the wire firmly into the foundation right through to the other side. Be sure to see that the end is tucked firmly back into the moss on the underside, so that your hands, the door or any other surface in contact with the garland, will not be scratched by exposed wires.

Wreath of pink roses

A Christmas chapeau (Photograph by courtesy of 'Woman's Journal')

senses, and a warm contrast to the chilly outside temperature.

FRONT-DOOR GARLAND

The basic colour scheme is green and scarlet, utilising the natural holly, variegated or plain, with its cheerful red berries. If there is a protective porch, you could also add a few chrysanthemum heads, otherwise it is better to leave out the fresh flowers. Other additions could include fir cones, suitably painted or glittered, colourful gourds, lacquered to keep them from withering, plus a few gay glass balls. All these accessories help to provide a very cheery welcome on a cold night. If your arrangement is destined to be used on an inner door, then you can include fresh flowers, wired firmly into the garland. Chrysanthemums and carnations will last well for a few days, and can always be renewed. Or you might prefer to use lovely flower heads preserved in borax, but only if the wreath is for indoor display.

A CHRISTMAS CHAPEAU

Here is a new use for an old beach hat, producing a splendid piece of Victorian headgear, which looks really charming on the door of a modern flat or house. First fill the crown with a mixture of detergent and water, made very stiff. Into this I thrust the materials of the 'feather boa': a gilded cycas leaf, and dried, bright yellow achillea flowers. Bright little glass baubles represent the fruit, so popular as a hat decoration in Victorian times. The non-drip flower candles are, of course, the 'hat-pins'. By the way, don't forget that when using detergent mixes as holders, one has to work fairly quickly, in order to complete the arrangement before the mix sets too hard.

CHRISTMAS DECORATIONS

These present a particular challenge, and another wonderful opportunity for creative expression. Employing all sorts of colourful and original materials, they can range from a natural, fairly simple arrangement, to something much more elaborate.

A CHRISTMAS BOUQUET

This could perhaps consist of some gilded leaves, fresh or dried, combined with chrysanthemums, in colours suitable to the season and the décor of your house. The traditional bright red of Christmas can be obtained through using tones of red and orange in the flowers you select. Such an arrangement as this is stimulating to the

CHRISTMAS LIGHTING IN BLUE AND WHITE

Even though these colours are cold and rather frosty in effect, and therefore should be used sparingly, they are traditionally employed in Christmas Nativity scenes. They also look simply lovely with candles and with the dried materials which you gathered from the woods, beaches and hedgerows during the summer, which can now be painted in gold or silver, blue or red. Incidentally, after painting your dried materials, and while they are still wet, shake them immediately in a paper bag containing matching or contrasting glitter. This halves your work, since once the paint has dried, the glitter will not adhere unless you first add a little picture varnish.

Silver glitter sprinkled on gold, white or blue paint is particularly effective, as is gold and red glitter sprinkled on white and red paint. The latter is really gorgeous, but you must also experiment with combinations of your own. And remember, using a paper bag for your glitter saves money as well as time, as by this means you avoid either spillage or waste.

OTHER CHRISTMAS IDEAS

Plain green leaves can be dressed up by lightly brushing them over with any good clean picture varnish, obtainable from any art shop. They can then be shaken in whatever colour glitter you fancy. Silver glitter, however, does give the most natural 'Jack Frost' look to plain leaves.

Lux flakes, shaken into a large mixing bowl, with a bare cup of cold water stirred in, and then spread on the branches and leaves of your Christmas tree, provide a most realistic effect of freshly fallen snow. If, in your enthusiasm, you do not make it stiff enough, some may fall to the floor, but you need not worry. It will not hurt the carpet, and if you just lightly brush it off all will be well. Another tip is to mix a detergent like Tide (a small packet) with two or three tablespoons of cold water, using this for the 'snow' instead of Lux. It sets harder, is less likely to fall or brush off, and looks almost as nice.

A CHRISTMAS ALL-ROUND DINNER TABLE ARRANGEMENT

A candlestick in silver is a most effective all-round arrangement for a formal Christmas dinner table. A candlecup is inserted into the top of the stick, held in position by Plasticine or a detergent (see page 22). Since preserved and dried materials are to be used no water is required, and a detergent such as Tide or Omo, or something similar, is the best fixative. A small packet of detergent, mixed with approximately two to three tablespoons of water to a very firm consistency, is the ideal flower holder for dried materials. Test it for strength. A stem placed in any position should be held quite firmly. If it starts drooping, the mixture is too soft, and you must add more detergent.

Now pack the candlecup with this mixture, pressing it well down, and level with the rim. If using a candle, insert it first and pack round it. You are then ready to begin the arrangement.

The materials are preserved beech leaves, dried figwort, and statice, silvered and sprinkled with blue glitter, dried natural blue-coloured dwarf eryngium, and dried pale blue hydrangeas, cut and preserved in their youth for the best results. Brush them lightly here and there with varnish and then immediately shake them first in silver, then in blue glitter, to emphasise their own delicate colouring. Shredded pampas grass is also used, but it does not require any paint and powder. In fact, it reacts by becoming horribly messy if you try to glamorise it. If it is left in its natural state and shredded lightly it provides a perfect foil for the painted and glittered materials, and also makes a colour link between the white candle and the pattern of the candlestick. It is really a most lovely addition to the arrangement, providing you shred it finely enough to suit the design. The completed arrangement, set on a shiny white damask cloth, with your best silver and cut glass and set off by blue and silver crackers at its base, would bring you much praise on Christmas night.

Another example of a Christmas mobile. It could be hung from a door, or free from a beam, with the back looking as attractive as the front. Sprays of evergreen in conjunction with strung beads, cones and some gay Shilosheen bows surround a candle

Here are bleached trails of amaranthus, and pieces of cloud-soft pampas grass. These preserved materials are combined with red skimmia berries and foliage, golden privet, and gold and tawny single chrysanthemums (the living materials) held in water. All surround a snowy candle in this Christmas composition

Flower lamp

An alternative all-round arrangement utilising some fresh materials would naturally require water in the candlecup holder. The candle should be inserted into the recess built for it within the candlecup and if a tighter fit is required, either slightly melt the base of the candle, thus waxing it into position, or press a little Plasticine around the base before any water is added. Place some wire netting inside the cup around the candle and commence the arrangement. Variegated dried foliage, dusted over with glitter, and the stems of bright berries and chrysanthemums are then inserted into the water. However, since this arrangement utilises both fresh and dried materials, the stems of the latter are better kept dry. Therefore, the amaranthus trails (love-lies-bleeding) and shredded pampas grass should be knitted into the wire netting, but held clear of the water. Of course, if glycerine-preserved foliage and flowers are used, it is immaterial whether the stems are placed in the water or not.

AN UNUSUAL CHRISTMAS LAMP

Tough long-lasting flowers like chrysanthemums and carnations are the best choice for this unique arrangement. They can live for quite a long while with their shortened and defoliated stems thrust into moist moss, provided they are given an initial twenty-four hours soak in deep water, and subsequently refreshed by an overall spray. To create the arrangement first roll a cylinder of 2-inch mesh, soft galvanised wire netting around the base of a cylindrically shaped table lamp. Roll it fairly tightly and fix it firmly at top and bottom with cut ends of the wire netting, or tie it with string. Now place generous handfuls of well-dampened moss the full length of the stand, securing it in position with another layer of wire netting. (If the stand is of polished wood, wrap a sheet of polythene around it first to protect it.) Tie the second wrap of wire netting in place, and you have a good foundation for your flowers and foliage.

Insert two or three well-chosen pieces of colourful ivy at the base. Twine them up and around the whole framework, pinning the stems in position here and there by florists' wire stubs bent over in half, like a hairpin. The two arms of the hairpin straddle the stem and hold it close to the framework. Choose your flowers and colours to blend with the preferably simple and unadorned lampshade, and insert their stems firmly into the moss with the aid of some more wire stubs. To do this the wire has to be looped around the calyx of the flower, then twisted along the stem, with a piece of wire protruding far enough to act as the pathfinder into the mossed foundation. In order to make the flowers extra secure, this end of wire can also be twisted back around a piece of the wire framework.

Such an arrangement takes up little space at a crowded party and is very eye-catching, especially when the lamp is lit. In the photograph, red and deep pink carnations were combined with bronze-tinted ivy to look perfectly delightful in the rosy glow from the red-shaded lamp.

A CHRISTMAS CANDLE

Imagine this candle glowing softly through glass, surrounded on the outside by short-stemmed red and white carnations, roses or chrysanthemums and set off by some dark evergreen foliage. If it is placed on a window-sill with curtains undrawn, so that its light shines against the darkness outside, it provides a welcoming touch for visitors and homecomers alike.

The flowers and foliage are held in crumpled chicken wire within a shallow bowl of water. Or, if you prefer, you can cut a ring of Oasis, and use it to hold the stems in position, remembering to keep it moist

For an all-dried or glycerined arrangement of flowers, berries, leaves, etc., you must now cut a round of Florafoam to fit the lantern base rather generously. Scoop out a hollow in the Florafoam for it to rest on. Then push into the protruding Florafoam the various stems of dried, painted and glittered Christmas materials. Strong stems like beech, figwort, oak and holly will go in unaided, but the delicate stems of fancy grasses, gilded bracken and fern will need to be strengthened with a twist of wire around their stems, by which you attach them to the base. For a lovely colour scheme, you could start with a bright flame-orange candle. One can buy the most attractive flame-shaped ones which look alight even when they are not! Add three short, full sprays of glycerined beech leaves, gilded and red-glittered, forming an outer skirt. Then three sprays of bracken (which could be silvered and glittered) are set between the beech, forming a secondary skirt. Follow these with clusters of bright red berries which are varnished to preserve them. Skimmia berries, if holly is not available, will do just as well. Small clusters of dried, painted and glittered quaking grass provide a little lightweight height, and transform the flat collar surrounding the lantern. In fact, with the grass added, this becomes a more elaborate and very colourful all-round arrangement which could even be used on a small Christmas dinner table. If you have three or four such lanterns, use them as the centrepiece of a large table. The arrangements could alternate between the unglittered fresh flowers and foliage and the brightly glittered preserved material.

Tiered flower baskets. For a special occasion, here are baskets galore piled on top of each other, filled with carnations, roses and anemone-centred asters, accompanied by trails of tradescantia, fern and rose foliage

A BUFFET OR FORMAL ARRANGEMENT

For any special occasion which requires extreme height, such as an official luncheon buffet, a tiered arrangement of flowers and foliage can be effective. The material is set in a succession of similar containers diminishing in size. In the picture, tin-lined baskets are attached to each other by contrived metal stands, and the flowers and foliage are arranged in crumpled 1½-inch mesh wire netting. The colour scheme is chosen to tone with the natural colour of the basket containers. To keep the edifice very steady one can (while everything is still dry) use a good chunk of Plasticine to fix the stand upon which the next basket will rest. For further safety, guide wires of string or wire can be tied from the inside rim of the basket on the top of each stand. These can be concealed by the flowers.

A FRUIT AND FLOWER ARRANGEMENT

For a refreshment trolley, or the sideboard from which dessert will be served, fruit combined with

a few flowers allows great scope. Fruit, ranging as it does from the heaviest textures to the comparative delicacy of the grape, is very definite in form and line and must be used boldly and imaginatively.

In the design on this page, pineapple, bananas and an orange are grouped with a strong feeling for textural similarity, at the base of a black wrought iron wine-server. This holds the candle-cup and is decorated with branches of leafy vine which, with its leaves and newly formed fruit, combines with a bunch of mature grapes to offer not only contrast of texture, but similarity of form. Remember, when you are using two dissimilar materials such as flowers and fruit, emphasis must be on one or the other. Here the emphasis is on the fruit, hence its setting near the drinks or dessert. The few gerbera flowers, chosen for their delicate strength and refinement, are in affinity with the grapes. They serve as the accent which completes this study of line and form. Their glowing colours, from palest apricot to tawny-orange, repeat the colours of the fruit beneath them, and unify the whole composition.

A fruit and flower arrangement

Pink and white larkspur, and four arum lilies are set against the strong background provided by the acanthus leaves, which is most essential for 'flower-pictures in a window', especially if the sun is shining

WINDOW ARRANGEMENTS

These, like flower arrangements for churches, have to be treated somewhat differently from the usual run of designs. The important thing to remember is that here you have a very strong background to contend with. Flowers do not show up well against the bright light of a window, unless you give them a strong built-in background. If using the design shown above, begin your arrangement with some low-placed, bold textured evergreen leaves, like megasea saxifrage, acanthus, chinensis aralia or ornopordum (anything broad and definite). With these you will set the general outline and cut out any disturbing background. Start arranging your flowers against these leaves, preferably using those of bold texture and colour, for they must be able to hold their own against dazzling sunlight.

33. *Christmas garland — a florist's wreath covered with moss and cupressus. Wired on to this base are colourful gourds, rosy crab apples, holly, and lacquered and frosted pine cones*

34. Sprays of white lilac form the arch of this fan-shaped design. Bold arum leaves provide 'body' and background for the definite shape of the arum flowers. White irises and stripped Portuguese laurel act as fillers

35. The very definite trumpet formation of King Alfred daffodils provides the required emphasis of form. The daffodils are used with the glossy evergreen foliage of V. Laurustinus, two branches only to each vase. Set in two typical narrow-necked altar vases, this is a mass arrangement rather than a line arrangement, which enables the flowers to hold their own against the ornate reredos

CHURCH FLOWER DECORATIONS

More and more interest is being taken by the average woman in beautifying churches with suitable altar and other flower arrangements. In a church, as with window-sill arrangements, one has to consider the background. But in this case it is not a strong light but a subdued light which provides difficulties for the unwary, as well as stained glass windows, handsomely carved pews, fluted columns and other magnificent effects. It is especially difficult to arrange the altar flowers if there happens to be an ornate reredos behind the altar. It is rather like a soloist in a concerto being overpowered by the orchestra instead of there being an harmonious partnership. A solid evergreen background should first be placed in position, and the flowers, buds, branches, berries and daintier leaves then arranged in the design of your choice. Place them more or less in front of this background, yet seeming to melt into it. Make your design whole and complete by careful attention to the three-dimensional placing of material, thus transforming it into one eye-catching flower picture, worthy of its setting in such majestic surroundings. The arrangement will show up well, especially if a grey-green foliage background (ornopordum leaves and artichoke leaves are ideal) is used in conjunction with light-reflecting tints of the advancing or warm colours. For example, use bright yellows and pastel pinks stemming from the pure orange hue rather than those coming from violet. White, with its high reflective power, is also an ideal choice, apart from its traditional use as a symbol of purity.

Early lilac, tulips, arum lilies and variegated aspidistra leaves make an effective Eastertime pedestal

This reredos in the little village church of Collaton-St.-Mary was commissioned by the express wish of the dying daughter of the Reverend Francis Lyte, author of the hymn 'Abide with Me'. It is very beautiful, but it is not easy effectively to arrange flowers to the glory of God beneath such overpowering artistry. Bold simple flowers set against a solid green background of foliage are the answer

Strong form in the flowers chosen is another helpful factor. Summer gladioli, lilies and acanthus flowers are bold and definite in outline, as are tulips and daffodils in spring. All these stand out and show up well from a distance, which is just what is required. Winter chrysanthemums are not quite so simple. Their rounded forms can merge into the background too easily. Look for really good foliage, with a clear-cut outline, such as phormium and yucca or dracena palm. Use it to break up the flowers, and render them more conspicuous. As a general rule more flowers are used for church arrangements than for a house decoration. However, as has already been stressed, form and design must stand out distinctly, and be discernible from a distance. The pedestal arrangement in colour plate 34, page 126 shows how effective this massing of good colour and form can be when it is placed against a solid background which has been built into the lower part of the arrangement. Bold arum leaves provide a solid background for the centrally placed lilies. Sprays of white lilac and defoliated Portuguese laurel form the spiky outlines and contrast of form. White irises act as fillers.

ALTAR VASE ARRANGEMENTS

Some people find the typical narrow-necked altar vases difficult to arrange satisfactorily. I agree they are not the easiest containers in which to arrange flowers, but with ingenuity they can be used to hold most attractive arrangements. The secret lies in careful wiring and choice of material. Use the minimum wire and leave many upturned ends protruding. Then select one large solid leaf or bract of foliage to provide the background. Use flowers of very definite sculptured shape and strong colour with stems as slim as possible. Select daffodils, gladioli or composite flowers like Michaelmas daisies and spray chrysanthemums which require vase room for only one stalk, and yet provide many heads. Such sprays will have to be judiciously trimmed if they are to follow a good line.

The two typical brass vases in the altar arrangement shown in colour plate 35, page 126 are designed first to attract your eye and then, through the flowing asymmetrical movement of their lines, to draw attention to the centrally placed cross, thus correctly fulfilling their destiny. If you have been asked to use lilies in altar vases remember they are bold flowers. Two or three at most, with one large leaf used artistically, will make an arrangement, and there is room for that number of thick stems in the narrowest vase. Moreover, you can tear a strip off arums. This makes them both thinner and more pliable, and also solves the problem of using church vases. Again, a candlecup holder could be fixed with Plasticine within the throat of a typical vase, thus providing more freedom of arrangement. However, care must be taken to ensure that the join between vase and candlecup is hidden by a placement of foliage and flowers. The arrangement must appear to be flowing from the vase itself. Once more, a greater number of flowers is used than would be the case if the arrangement was created for a house.

AN ALTAR ARRANGEMENT

A very ornate reredos behind the altar on page 128 compelled me to keep the arrangement low. The horizontal design was therefore the best choice, relying upon the elongated sideways sweep to give it good proportion. The reredos is cut out of a natural cream stone, weathered to a somewhat deeper hue. The materials were chosen with both its colour and texture in mind.

Some of the regale lilies were turned to show more of the purplish veining, others angled frontwards to reveal their pale yellow throats, and the daisies with their cheekily bright yellow centres were set against the green foliage. Used in this manner, they offered sufficient contrast to each other in their tonal values of colour, to enable the arrangement to hold its own. The daisies were used to accentuate the curving rhythm of the design which builds up to the Cross in the centre. The arrangement and the Cross do not detract from each other. Although distinctive, they are not separate entities but are unified with the Cross as the dominant factor. This, of course, should always be the case when creating church altar arrangements.

Wedding bells are ringing, and their mood is reflected in the four pure white galtonias and six white and gold-splashed regale lilies. This sculptured perpendicular arrangement, held in Oasis in an alabaster urn, combines purity of colour and line. Silvery begonia leaves and a shimmering piece of gold lamé emphasise the principle of unity

WEDDING ARRANGEMENTS

Wedding flowers follow the same general principles as church decorations. Although white is the traditional colour, it is becoming increasingly popular to introduce pastel tints to harmonize with the bride's dress or bouquet, or to use her favourite colour.

The soft greeny-blue of some hydrangeas, arranged with a little silver-grey foliage and a lot of white, looks delightful for a summer wedding. Pale pinks and white give a warmer feeling for earlier or later in the year. Swags of greenery, wired into mossed frame or garlands, can be hung beside the entrance to each pew. Window-sills can be treated as if they were mantelpieces with lavish 'skirted' arrangements and not too much superstructure. All such decorations will add to the splendour of this all-important occasion.

At the reception, concentrate the flowers in just two prominent places. The first should be beside the bride, where she and the groom stand to receive their guests. For preference it should be a pedestal arrangement such as in colour plate 23, page 93. In this pedestal I used many more flowers and much less foliage than for the other pedestals, for, as in church arrangements which have to compete with an elaborate background, the bride may be standing against a window or in the centre of a large room. Also there will be many people moving to and fro, making a kaleidoscope background, which will further distract attention from the design.

The second lavish arrangement at a reception should be on the bride's table. A low, elaborated oval all-round arrangement is best for a sit-down meal. For a buffet table the flowers should be planned to complement the cake. A tiered cake is usually a rather stately affair, so to be in keeping with it, the textural quality of the flowers should be somewhat heavier. The design of the arrangement can be quite elaborate, especially if the cake is rather plain. On the other hand, if the cake itself is very much decorated, the flower design must be kept fairly simple, and would be best executed in materials of more delicate texture.

CONTAINERS
Their practical and aesthetic value

Baking tins can hold flowers as well as cakes!

Types and Uses

By the term container we mean anything capable of holding flowers, foliage and associated materials in water. Should the width or diameter of a container be greater than its height, it is known as a bowl, irrespective of whether it is round, oval or rectangular. If the height is the dominant measurement, then it is technically a vase. Plain colours and simple elegance of line make the best containers for either simple or elaborate arrangements. Among the most useful are flat oblong pottery bowls, with or without little legs, and urn-shaped pedestal types in metal, pottery or china. Ordinary round mixing bowls which can be used in conjunction with a stand are suitable for pedestal arrangements. In such an arrangement the container is hardly glimpsed, owing to the nature of the arrangement. Its colour must not be obtrusive and its depth should be sufficient for a quantity of thirsty stems ($4\frac{1}{2}$ to 5 inches). It is also essential that it has a flat bottom to hold the pin-holder firmly.

Driftwood and candlecup combine to make an unusual container

Jugs of various dimensions make charming holders, particularly for the more old-fashioned summer garden or wild flowers. Copper trays can act as bases combined with matching small bowls or camouflaged cream jars, or you can use cut-down and painted tins.

Hyacinth-bulb bowls are also very useful for a summer arrangement. As they are semi-porous, they act as coolers or refrigerators, and this helps to prolong the lives of our delightful but often short-lived summer flowers. All metal containers share this same quality, and achieve the same result, because they breathe. Silver, lead, wrought iron and pewter have the added advantage of giving an impression of coolness, and therefore play a useful part in summertime arrangements. Copper and brass, while still keeping the arrangement cool, evoke a sense of warmth in the eye of the beholder, owing to their colour value. Pieces of beach driftwood, roots of fallen trees, pieces of polished marble (perhaps the broken bits of a washstand) could all be made into the most attractive containers for the more aristocratic flowers of the garden. Equally attractive are the unpolished, crazy-paving marble pieces which can be found in delightful muted tones and are particularly suitable for our humbler flowers. All these can give great pleasure in both the finding and the fashioning. They also add that touch of originality, an elusive quality which is so prized in any design.

Some of my flower containers: the usual urns and vases, and the more unusual finds from antique shops and markets down to commonplace things about the house like salad bowls, compote dishes, candlesticks, jugs and bottles which can lead a double life in our homes

Once the party is over, a dimple Scotch bottle is too precious to lie idle. Rose stems and thorns look attractive under water. These few stems require no more than a tight fit at the neckline to keep them in place

A cut-and-growing arrangement. The golden forsythia branches, daffodils and hart's tongue fern are arranged on a pinholder, while the polyanthus and primroses are complete with their roots just trailing in the water

Avoid using clear glass containers, even though they are very attractive. You should know the reason why I say this from what you have already learned about the designing and constructing of a flower arrangement. Remember one of the five basic rules — that all stems should spring from a given position. The criss-cross of stems below that given point, plus any wire netting or other mechanics, if visible below the waterline, will quite spoil the beauty of line which you have so carefully created above. Once I found myself devoting an entire lesson to the subject of glass containers. I had suggested a lesson on difficult containers, and my class greeted the idea with great enthusiasm. When I arrived the following week I was met with an amazing conglomeration of long and narrow-necked, short and wide-mouthed and elegant specimen vases — one and all in glass! By the end of that particular class I will admit that I had grown positively fond of them.

However, if you do possess clear glass containers it is not necessary to throw them away. Try brushing them over with a light coating of emulsion paint or distemper, using pastel tints to match your room and materials. Containers thus treated will become most useful additions to your collection. The paint washes off quite easily when a change of colour is required and also completely masks the conflicting underwater lines.

CLEAR GLASS, especially cut glass, which it would be criminal to paint, can occasionally be used very successfully. The narcissi family, and other natural water lovers, look very graceful with the natural association of their stems and water. This type of arrangement, however, must be arranged in a very simple style. It can either be grouped in one hand and eased into the vase with the other, or placed in position on a table, bound invisibly with a 'twistit', and then inserted in the container. After arranging, the stems should be cut to different lengths and so manoeuvred into position that they fan out gracefully under water, in a simple design of their own. Roses, too, can be arranged like this. Their colourful stems and thorns become even more beautiful with the water acting as an enchanting magnifying-glass.

Always link the shape of your container with the design of your arrangement. For example, a pedestal vase looks perfect if it is used as the 'handle' of fan-shaped arrangement. It would also lend itself to a drooping pyramid.

CANDLESTICKS, in all their variety, from wood, brass and copper to the stateliest of Georgian silver candelabra make wonderful containers. I possess a favourite blue and white Delft candlestick, bought for only ten shillings when rummaging in an antique shop. Candlesticks must be fitted with candlecups, obtainable from most florists. Paint the cups to tone with the candlestick, and press into the candle aperture, using a little Selastik, Plasticine or even Tide, to hold it firm. Candlesticks are just the thing for that most peaceful of designs, the horizontal, or all-round buffet table arrangements. They are, however, a little tall when correctly arranged for a sit-down meal.

A horizontal movement by one of my first-year students. A well-executed design, although a little overpowered by the candlestick. It would have been better if Miss Johnson had remembered to lower her arrangement in order to cover the candlecup at the top of the candlestick, thus reducing its overall length and importance as a container, and making it subordinate to the flowers

NATURAL SHELLS, with their delightful colouring and unusual shapes, provide much scope for original design. One can make up a container from two or three shells put together with plaster of Paris, thus creating something quite original. This type of container is particularly useful when attempting a more unusual design for competition work.

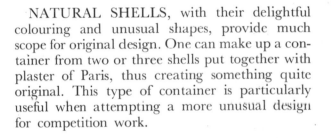

Shells from the seashore make an apt accessory for the shell vase. Its frilly skirt repeats the pattern of the frilled floribunda roses. Dainty larkspur spikes break up any excessive roundness in the composition

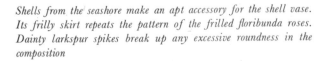

Soft pink spikes of astilbe, pink larkspur and deeper pink roses in a stark diagonal design

The blue-green sea-snail shell shown on page 132, especially when combined with a marble base, suggests an asymmetrical arrangement. However, beware of using anything but medium-textured materials (preferably in soft colourings), such as indeterminate blues, grey-greens and mauves, to harmonise with the ocean atmosphere.

THE CONTAINER AS AN INSPIRATION

For elegant or sophisticated arrangements, visit your silver cupboard or china shelves. Roses in silver or pewter are almost hackneyed, but nevertheless truly elegant. Part of the secret is the complete harmony this combination creates. Also, metal containers tend to exclude the summer heat, and with quick-fading flowers like roses this is another link to keep them together. Certainly, the use of a metal container will help to keep your arrangement cooler, and in a hot show tent or on a warm sunny day at home this is important.

If you have a yearning to use a particular piece of patterned china, be sure to link up and harmonise the colours of your flowers and greenery with the pigment tones of your china. Pick up and repeat the dominant colour in the container for your focal point. Such a galaxy of colour would be particularly suitable for a teenage party, setting just the right tempo for a gay time.

Golden roses and their foliage in a golden incense burner sweep in a graceful curve towards the lid, which is being used as an accessory both to maintain correct visual balance and lend interest

Low containers like this attractive cigarette box are perfect for the regal iris. These deep purple blooms, grouped so that each flower can be shown off to perfection, are held in place with a heavy rectangular pin-holder. Holder is placed inside a concealed bowl of water

A wedding conjures up a vision of white flowers, because white symbolises peace, purity and delicacy. The container to complement them, and to continue the theme, could be a fluted oval vase, or one of the various types of urn in white pottery or china. For example, how charming a fan-shaped arrangement would be, using white delphiniums to form the ribs of the fan. Sprays of sweet scented philadelphus (mock orange), much defoliated and trimmed to preserve an uncluttered line and to ensure longevity, could be used between the ribs as a background. Pure-looking regale or arum and longifolium lilies could be placed in the foreground. Three large Peace roses could provide the focal point.

A christening suggests a round font-type bowl as the natural choice. Use an alabaster one, if you possess such a treasure, or a silver one. You could create an all-round arrangement using innocent-looking white chincherinchees and larkspur, dainty, creamy-white and pastel-tinted freesias, and small rounded clusters of the tiny butter-yellow banksia rose combined with silver-grey foliage.

On a hectic day soothe yourself with the tranquillising influence of a Japanese type arrangement based upon the modern Moribana style of Japan. One of those flat oblong containers on little feet is an ideal choice. Or you might use a slab of marble in conjunction with driftwood. The stark simplicity of the traditional asymmetrical triangle, with the arrangement created at one end of the dish leaving an expanse of water, is very placating to frayed nerves. It can be cooling too, if executed in pale tints and tones.

Brass and copper play a useful part in accentuating the gaiety of late summer and early autumn, mixing merrily with the autumnal colours. In this case you could utilise a made-up container, consisting of a round copper or brass tray, with a matching ashtray to actually hold the arrangement. Otherwise, a substitute container will do: something which can be hidden by discreetly placed foliage or a large flower. A crescent design,

being itself a half-circle, would repeat the rhythm of the circular tray. For materials, the strong yellows and orange of French marigolds or zinnias would blend well with the metal. Combine them with beech leaves turned golden, after their drink in glycerine-water, and perhaps some natural mahogany-coloured foliage, such as the copper beech and Prunus pisardii. Such colours suggest and prolong a sense of warmth and well being.

A play on elliptical shapes is shown in this gay crescent of red and orange zinnias, accompanied by autumn-tinted beech and yellow achillea

much the centre of attraction, great care should be taken over its selection. While in harmony with its surroundings and the flowers it is containing, it must nevertheless be quite sturdy in itself and well balanced. Could anything worse happen to a hostess than to see a flood of water cascading all over her immaculate cloth, with flowers strewn in its path — all because somebody inadvertently jogged the table and the container could not survive the shock! The period and colour of the table, the room itself, the tablecloth or mats — all these are important factors in creating a completely unified composition which is eminently suitable for the particular occasion.

The more sophisticated delicate types of floral materials, such as orchids, freesias and fern, are shown to advantage in elegant silver or delicate china or cut glass containers, particularly for a dinner-party. Coarser heavy textured flowers like zinnias and marigolds, dahlias and geraniums or even daffodils, with their stronger colouring and heavier texture, are more suitable for breakfast or luncheon tables. They are also more at home in pottery containers, or in a finely fashioned wooden nut-bowl or jug if it corresponds to the wood of the table.

CONTAINERS AND TEXTURES

Always check the visual weight of a container with the flowers and foliage you are about to use. Heavy wrought iron or similar metal, especially if left in their natural sober hues which add to their weight value, must be used with correspondingly strong foliage. Magnolia, laurustinus in their many varieties, mahonia and flowers like roses and tulips are a good choice. Peel the tulip leaves as you would a banana, and they assume a most attractive sculptured look and help to form a stepping stone or bridge between the heavy-looking container and the fairly delicate flower. Gladioli, roses and most lilies also combine well.

For dinner-tables, where the container is so very

A mixed fruit salad, a hot coffee and some cheerful daffodils in this cheeky little container should clear the Black Monday mood

CONTAINERS AND SCALE

In addition to checking the texture of your container with the plant material arranged in it and ensuring that they blend harmoniously, there is also the important principle of scale to bear in mind. This is the size relationship between *all* the component parts. Choose large flowers and foliage for large arrangements in big containers and smaller flowers and leaves for moderately sized arrangements in an average-sized container.

For miniature work do be absolutely sure to use completely whole flowers. Nothing is more distressing to a flower judge than to see portions of flowers and leaves used in an effort to scale down large material to fit a minute container. Look for the perfect and complete small or miniature flower, such as a miniature rose. Saxifrage and sedums in variety also offer plenty of scope.

THE CONTAINER AND ITS BASE

Very often it enhances an arrangement to set the container upon a piece of wood or slab of marble. This is known as a base or supplementary part of a container. If used, it is always considered an integral part of the design, and the dimensions are calculated to include it.

This excellent symmetrical triangle design, utilising golden preserved beech, coral pink begonias and gladioli, and anemones, was created by one of my third-year students. In this arrangement Mrs. Chapman reveals her strong grasp of good design and the principles of flower arrangement. However, the container is a little too ethereal. Wood or pottery would have been texturally more in keeping with the flowers

Leucothoe, shredded pampas grass, chrysanthemums and grapes in a hamper basket give the impression they could actually have travelled inside it

FUNCTIONAL CONTAINERS

Teapots, beer mugs, wine servers, copper kettles picked up in antique shops, jugs of various sizes, from utilitarian pottery in daily use to exotic Eastern pewter pitchers, can all be employed for floral display. Hamper baskets also come within the above heading.

When deciding to use them, make quite sure that the container and materials to be used blend together happily as regards texture and colouring. Before planning the design recall to mind the original and intended function of the jug or kettle. Then design an arrangement which emphasises that function. But let me explain in more detail.

A jug or pitcher usually possesses a handle and a pouring lip. You use it by holding the handle and pouring liquid from the lip, or spout as in the case of a kettle. To see you doing otherwise would create a feeling of discomfort in any beholder. Similarly, when arranging flowers in such vessels, utilise your tall, more erect materials in following the upward emphasis of the handle, letting your curvaceous, shorter materials appear to pour from the lip or spout. The over-all design could be in the shape of an asymmetrical triangle, or a diagonal or a Hogarth curve (the lazy 'S', executed fairly upright). These shapes will emphasise the intended function, and provide the beholder with a sense of rhythm and unity (see colour plate 11,

page 52). A hamper basket of flowers, such as the one on this page, should be designed to suggest its function of conveying things. Many varied designs can be employed, such as the pyramid (symmetrical triangle), the crescent, the asymmetrical triangle, the horizontal movement and many others. One should however restrict oneself

A Hogarth curve executed by third-year student Mrs. Brooking, who declared she had not mastered this tricky design. Her excellent arrangement proves the reverse! The strong movement of this flowing line design has its emphasis on the function of the container. An upward movement over the handle, established by one curving gladiolius in bud and some cytisus (broom), with a pouring complementary movement over the spout, and the placement of the roses follows the line pleasingly

A way of using a few left-over flowers. Off-white anemones and paper-white narcissi reflect the colouring of the sleeping swan

to the simpler flowers and foliage, those types which would most likely be packed in just such a basket. More exotic blooms and foliage would travel differently, and therefore should be left out of a basket or hamper arrangement.

In this type of arrangement, the great thing to bear in mind is that your proportions are arrived at differently. Instead of making sure you have adequate height by measuring and cutting one stem to at least one and a half times the length of the hamper (its greatest measurement), you go by the diagonal of the hamper and allow just a little more. This then becomes the measurement of your tallest stem, ensuring that the finished arrangement appears to 'fit its box', rather like one of those pop-up pictures in a child's story book: when opened they appear a little larger than the book that contains them. Yet if you close the book they disappear inside. This, of course, is asking too much of a flower arrangement! Nevertheless, if you do not extend your measurements too much, the observing eye will be happily deceived into accepting the union of beauty and purpose.

OTHER BASKETS
Any basket with a handle, such as garden trugs, falls into this general category. There is also a far better way of using them than for their intended function, which is merely to hold the garden material temporarily as they are cut and that is to use them as an extremely attractive container. If you look at the florist's gypsy basket on page 11, and the little round one on this page which holds just a few cyclamen flowers and leaves, you will see that such arrangements should be so designed that the handle is clearly seen. It does not need to be quite as much on view as in the little round arrangement, but it is an essential part of the basket, and because of that it should be visible and usable.

SWANS, DONKEY CARTS and other such nonsense-pieces should again be treated with careful thought. Work out your design in relation to the story you want the finished picture to convey. For example, the flowers arranged on the swan's back could be in a swept-back design so as to resemble its own stately wings. For the donkey cart you might try a low round design with emphasis on groups of little flowers, like types and colourings together, using a polychromatic colour scheme. This, with grey foliage to help blend the various hues, will present a happy picture of a wayside flower seller.

No matter what its shape, flowers can be found which will complement your container perfectly. The half-finished arrangement of roses illustrates the beautiful contrast of velvet petals and porcelain

Cyclamens in a basket. The handle is correctly left clear and uncluttered in the design

Lupins will *curve, so use these bends to create a lovely Hogarth curve, aided in this case by three curvaceous delphiniums. Two roses and stachys lanata flower heads fill in the design, and a begonia flower is supported at the focal point by seven stachys lanata leaves*

Whatever type of container you are using, whether it be simple or elaborate, conventional or unorthodox, keep the following points in mind:

Plan your entire composition beginning with the container.

Visualise in your mind's eye what you intend doing, and then do it.

Do not be afraid to try out new ideas.

Employ your knowledge of the mechanics and principles of flower arranging.

Relax and be creative!

36. *A piece of driftwood in front of a well-pinholder forms the container for this dried-and-living arrangement. Glycerine-preserved azara microphylla (which turns almost black), one deeply lobed aralia chinensis leaf and a small pair of eucalyptus leaves provide the permanent background to a changing scene of flowers. Here yellow dahlias add a bright contrast*

37. *A zigzag design inspired by the root, which is used as the container. Preserved beech leaves and bronze chrysanthemums emphasise the colour link, with a still-green mahonia bealei leaf striking a note of contrast*

VIII HOW TO CHOOSE AND LOOK AFTER YOUR MATERIALS

Good health and long life to our flowers!

With practice, doing the flowers need not take up too much of the busy housewife's time, particularly when she has learned how to create long-lasting arrangements. Because, no matter how much we may enjoy flower arranging, few of us have the time to be for ever creating new designs or touching up finished ones which have begun to show signs of age. And there is nothing more disappointing, if you have taken a great deal of trouble with a design, if it almost immediately begins to droop and fade.

For all these reasons, one of the most important aspects of the art of flower arranging is to learn how to take care of your materials. In the present chapter you will find all the best methods for choosing, cutting and maintaining fresh flowers and foliage. You will also learn some really exciting techniques of long-term preservation which will enable you to always have wonderful materials at hand, no matter how inclement the season.

WHEN CUTTING FRESH FLOWERS AND FOLIAGE

Always pick them late in the evening, after sundown. The sap in the plants recedes with the departure of the sun, and for this reason materials picked at this time of the day last much longer. After the various initial treatments described below, plunge the flowers into a bucket of cool water which has been placed in a dark draught-free cool place, and leave them to soak overnight.

INITIAL TREATMENT FOR CUT FLOWERS AND FOLIAGE

Bruise or crush the stems of all woody materials like chrysanthemums, and all shrubs and evergreens, before plunging into the bucket.

A bract of laurustinus aucuba foliage, mahonia bealei foliage, two sprays of broom and two autumnal coloured chrysanthemums are arranged in a tall modern goblet. The simplicity of the design makes it suitable for a writing-desk

Cut between the joints of carnations and pinks and similar stems. If cut at the joint they do not absorb water so readily.

Separate the foliage from the flowering branches of woody shrubs like lilacs, philodelphus and weigelia. If you want the flowers to last, soak the branches with leaves separately from the branches with the flower stems. In fact, the branches bearing the leaves only, if of new growth, would benefit from total immersion in a cold bath for a few hours.

Hydrangeas should be cut and kept on the well-bruised main stem. Make sure, however, that it is only moderately old wood. If it is too woody or very new and soft, the flowers will fade much sooner.

PARTIAL DEFOLIATION of most flower stems, to a greater or lesser extent, is a necessary precaution, because this reduces the rate of transpiration (evaporation of water) through the leaves. If the evaporation exceeds the amount of water entering the flower stem, early wilting and death of the blooms is certain. Flowers wilt because they are not receiving enough water. It is to prevent, or at least postpone, this happening that partial defoliation and the various treatments of the stem end are recommended. Also, both when the flowers are soaking overnight and when arranged, keep them out of draughts and away from excessive heat. Both these conditions tend to hasten the process of excessive transpiration.

ENTIRE DEFOLIATION is the best way of preserving the long-lasting chrysanthemum. For one thing, the flower invariably outlasts the leaf, sometimes by several weeks. If one relied upon the leaves as part of the arrangement, the whole design would have to be redone within a short time. Whereas if one substitutes some suitable evergreen foliage on separate stems the whole arrangement will last about four or five weeks, depending on the original state of the flowers. Defoliation of all stems below water level is essential if algae (bacterial growth) are to be prevented and the arrangement kept sweet.

NON-WOODY STEMS

Slit the stems and cut at an angle to prevent them adhering closely to the bottom of the container, thus cutting off their supply of water. If you remember that the cut end of a flower stem is its

Ornithogalum lacteum, commonly known as the chincherinchee, a native of South Africa, is a most uncommonly long-lasting flower. In an arrangement dominated by them and Rex begonia leaves it is the leaves which will require pepping-up by a good soak, while understudies take their places. If, however, these flowers and sansevieria leaves were used together, then the whole arrangement would last for a considerable time, with no attention needed except to top up the water

main way of obtaining refreshment, you will do this automatically.

HOLLOW STEMS
Flowers of this type, such as lupins, should be up-ended and force-fed with the aid of a medicine dropper. Go slowly with this process to make sure no air bubbles form, thus cheating the stem of its full drink. When the flower is filled to capacity a finger should be placed over the cut end and the stem and finger immersed in the pail of water. Once the stem is in the water you can remove your finger again. On the following morning when arranging flowers which have been treated in this way, cut them to the required lengths underwater, if possible, then plug the stem end with a minute piece of cotton wool. This helps to retain the water in the stem and you can then arrange your flowers secure in the knowledge that they will not flag. Should it be necessary to recut the stems after removing from the pail, do so with the stem end upwards, and replug at once.

FLESHY STEMS
Flowers like anchusa, anemones and polyanthus should be recut when they are plunged into the bucket of water. This releases any air bubbles which may have formed and to which these varieties are so prone. Tulips also like this treatment, but it is not so essential in their case. Indeed, when flowers are arranged, air bubbles are the chief cause of their flagging.

STEMS WHICH BLEED
Poppies, bocconia, poinsettias, heliotropes and euphorbia, and other similar types, give off a milky fluid or juice. They must have their stem ends burnt or singed either with a candle flame, or in a gas jet, or best of all by a red-hot coal. Then they should be plunged into the bucket of cold water for their long soak. When arranging them the next day, if you want to recut the stems, remember to burn the fresh-cut ends again, before placing them in the container.

HOT-WATER TREATMENT
This is necessary for the globe artichoke leaf stem and beetroot and acanthus leaves, but not for their flower stem. It also greatly prolongs the lives of the helleborus niger (Christmas rose) and helleborus orientalis (Easter flowering), and, to a lesser extent, the corsica variety (the all-green) dahlias, and other such flowers. In fact, neither of the heleborus will stand up at all without such treatment. Cut their stems at a slant and plunge them into the hot water. Protect the flowers and leaves from the steam by placing a plastic bag over them, tying it loosely midway down the stems.

Wilting flowers can also be helped by the hot-water treatment, providing they are basically fresh and only suffering from the effects of being out of water for a little while, or from being in a draught or overheated. May I also make the point, that if properly treated flower or foliage stem looks wilted before its time, check on the water level in the container. If it has receded below the level of the individual stem, remove that stem; before topping up, treat the stem according to its own requirements: Then plunge it into hot water as described above, leaving it to cool before replacing it in the arrangement. All stems given this hot-water treatment may be either left to cool off in the same water or transferred to an arrangement after an hour or two.

Acanthus is beloved by both architects and sculptors (its leaf served as a model for designs used in the ornamentation of Corinthian architecture). It is here arranged in a battery jar. The leaves must be given very hot water to drink, for about five minutes before arranging

Pink tulips, silvery pussy-willow and chlorophytum leaves are arranged in a maroon-lined grey salad dish

them after arranging — and what a great blessing that is!

Bulbous plants, such as narcissi and others, particularly tulips, which are typified by 'simple entire' leaves, require only a little water in their final containers. Anything more than 3 inches of water at the most will cause a disaster. A tulip, for instance, will topple like a drunk over the edge of the container! Should this happen* retrieve the flowers, keep them out of water till quite limp then roll them in a 'straight-jacket' of graphite or greaseproof paper. Cut the ends of the stem which are now sealed and replace them in shallow water. When quite stiff again, remove the paper and the flower should be like a ramrod!

Tearing a strip off arum lilies in particular, and to some extent, most fleshy thick-stemmed plants, can be a great help. The process does them no injury, providing it is not carried to excess. Beside making the thick stem smaller, it also has quite a wonderful and little-known stabilising effect upon tulips and anemones, helping to immobilise

* NOTE: This will also happen with the onset of old age and then the recommended treatment will not apply. However, do not discard the flowers. Use them in another design, incorporating their graceful curves, which can be most useful for the front skirt of a pedestal arrangement.

A delightfully simple fan design, just using tulips and their own foliage

The root of an old tree forms the unusual and attractive container for this all-foliage arrangement. Two colourful begonia leaves cover the pinholder in a small water container and provide the focal point of the arrangement, making a striking foil for the wild iris leaves, pussy willow, hart's tongue fern and chlorophytum rootlets

Soak house-plant leaves like the Rex begonias, ivies etc., by laying them flat on the surface of the water in a basin for a few hours. After this treatment, they should survive many hours in an arrangement, although, in the case of begonias, it is useful to be equipped with some spares.

WILD FLOWERS
Some, like valerian and many leaves like *iris foetidissima* and hart's tongue will outlast garden flowers if cut, their stems crushed and popped into a bucket of water at once and kept out of a draught.

An alternative method is to place them in an airtight plastic bag, previously sprinkled with water, until such time as they can be transferred to a bucket for their long cool drink before arrangement.

In early spring when flowers are definitely conspicuous by their absence try a 'cut and growing' arrangement. Two or three branches just burgeoning into leaf are impaled upon a pinholder which is placed within a long, comparatively shallow container. This one was made for me in lead by my husband. Three precious stems of early forced iris are the only cut materials, the few early polyanthus and primroses have been removed bodily from their beds, roots and all. After careful washing of their lower roots, which reach into the water in the container, the clumps are planted, just on or preferably above the water level in the 'rockery', which conceals the pinholder from whence the other materials spring. The rich glowing colours of the polyanthus provide a glorious focal point, and the little earth that disintegrates into the water is hardly discernable amongst the stones and against this 'natural' container. Such an arrangement lasts for some weeks, and then the clumps of polyanthus and primroses can be replanted in the garden

Bronze and yellow chrysanthemums and some rosemary foliage held on a pinholder follow a gracious Hogarth curve complementing this rather exotic bronze compote. Rosemary is very stiff and will not bend, but fortunately the bushes grow with many a natural curve and twist. Seek these and use them to fullest advantage to establish a good and interesting line design

Good specimens of incurving disbudded chrysanthemums. The top one in the foreground has reached its zenith of 'rotundity' — its neighbour, still slightly flat, has a little way to go. The chrysanthemums in the lower picture are at their zenith

WHEN BUYING FLOWERS

Always look for turgidity of stem and leaves. Just as freshly washed hair crackles under its final rinse, so should the leaves and stems of freshly picked flowers. This is especially true of tulips. Incidentally, the tulip flower should emerge just clear of its leaves on a moderately tall stem. If it appears to have outgrown its clothes, the flower head appearing some six inches or more above the top leaf, it is likely that the flower has been overforced, and will not hold up well.

With daffodils and other narcissus, always look at the tip of the petals. If they appear to be at all papery and transparent look for some fresher ones. Remember that closed buds will open and last longer. The condition of the bottom of the stems will also tell a tale of freshness or otherwise to the discerning eye, in the case of most annuals and perennials handled by florists. Arums and regale lilies should have a velvet bloom right to the tips of the petals, and if you run a finger gently under their curving edges they should be firmly resistant. If slack, they are not in their first prime.

Chrysanthemums should be judged by their varieties. In the case of singles, you look to the tell-tale stem end before the florist cuts it off. You can also judge the general condition of the flower by the freshness of the leaves and opaque petals. The 'eye' should be tight and firm, as with scabious. Both these flowers should have a centre which is tight and button-like, not feathery.

Decorative chrysanthemums, both the reflex and incurving varieties, are judged first by the leaves. Is the underside of the leaves a good clean colour? Are they firm? Then study the petals. If they are clear and unmarked, with a crisp look about them, you can be sure they are good blooms. Please do not be put off by the reflex action of the petals of the reflex varieties: chief of these, the gorgeous Favourites, often receive undeserved disparagement from would-be purchasers who do not know their habits. These, and all the reflex varieties of flowers, are possessed of petals which curl backwards and downwards, as well as those which are furled tightly over faces. So long as the reflexed petals are in good condition and their faces are tightly bandaged, the flowers will last and last. In fact, for sheer graceful beauty and long-lasting quality, I would choose a Favourite every time.

The other variety, the incurving, can be best judged for age by the condition of their 'figures'. Are they round and plump, a lovely ball of white, yellow or bronze, with no flattening of the perimeter opposite the calyx? If this is the case they are at their zenith, and although they will last some time because they are a hardy race, they will not last as long as if you bought them when slimmer, with a distinct flattening of the 'tummy'. The process of increasing rotundity, if I may express it thus, will go on in your vase and you will have better value for your money.

TO KEEP WATER FRESH

I am always being asked about aids to freshening the water in which flowers are placed. Sugar may help in some cases to revive flowers that are suffering from the effects of a draught. Flowers in copper containers benefit from the effect of the metal, and therefore copper compounds in the water are sometimes beneficial. To prevent the formation of bacteria, especially in the case of dirty-stemmed flowers like asters, a lump of charcoal in the water works wonders. It absorbs the bacteria and keeps the water fresh.

Frequent changes of water are desirable in all arrangements, especially the longlasting ones. However, it is not advised that you disarrange the flowers, rather that you should take the arrangement bodily to the sink and allow the tap to run freely into the container and overflow. Continue this until the water from the container runs sweet and clear. Place the arrangement on the draining board for a time, or on a wooden table, to let it dry off, and then return it to its former position nicely refreshed.

So much for specialised treatment to ensure longevity. Now we will proceed to discuss the drying and preserving of some of the garden's produce. Many flowers, and a lot of evergreen, can be kept from one season to the next by one of three methods: air-drying, water-drying, and by use of glycerine and water combined. Flower heads can also be preserved in borax.

DRYING AND PRESERVING

Air-drying: The stems of materials which are to be preserved in this fashion must never go near water. The flower stems are defoliated (unless the leaves are particularly required) and are then hung head downwards in a warm spot, preferably in a current of air, and allowed to dry off until required for use. An airing cupboard, with the door left open after the first couple of days, is the ideal. Chlorophytum leaves, especially when cut with rootlets attached, the acanthus flower spike, the agapanthus (blue African lily), delphinium spikes, larkspur and all fancy grasses, should be cut when young and fresh, and dried in this way. Seed heads of nigella (love-in-a-mist), physalis (Chinese lanterns), the colourful dock seed heads, figwort and other attractive wayside weeds may also be preserved in this manner. They are most useful for autumn flower arrangements, or for use, gilded and tinselled, for Christmas arrangements. Catananche, helichrysum, and lunaria (honesty) also adapt well to this method.

Water-drying: Certain flowers like to dry off

gradually with their stems in water, retaining a better colour and seeming to do better by this method. The hydrangea family takes particularly well to this treatment. If the flowers to be dried off are freshly picked, young and of good colour, they should be arranged in a vase with the usual amount of water, and then the arrangement placed high above a radiator or near a fireplace. Do not top it up with water. The flowers will become most wonderfully preserved, and can be used later in the autumn or even in the winter. Others of this family (especially the Marshall Foch variety which turn brick-red on the plant itself, and remain so until late in the season) may be left and gathered then, and merely air-dried as above. Achilleas (yarrow family) take kindly to the water-drying treatment, and they last even longer than the hydrangeas (I have had some for two years), but do not use the heat treatment with these. Eryngium (sea holly) is another plant which gives good service if it is first placed in water and given time to dry out in the vase. It can then be put away for autumn and winter use.

Glycerine-Water Solution: Use in equal parts and mix well together. Immerse the stems only (after thoroughly crushing in the case of 'woodies' and a slanting cut in others), to about 4 or 5 inches in

A heavy metal urn, its colouring matched by the three bullrushes which are arranged in bold upright design, holds in addition a heavy textured red gladioli, its leaves, variegated foliage and rose and begonia flowers

Stems of larkspur preserved in glycerine-water solution cohabit with late blooming summer flowers in an urn full of water. The hydrangeas can be allowed to dry out gradually in such an arrangement as the water level recedes from their stems and is not topped-up. They, too, will then be preserved for future use in good heart and colour

depth. Make sure, within the first twenty-four hours or so, that they still have enough liquid, and top up with the same mixture if required. Then leave them for some two to four weeks, varying with the types of materials. When ready, remove and store away from dust, in a well-ventilated cupboard or shelf, till required. Materials so preserved require no further fussing and are quite happy, either with other fresh materials in water or arranged dry.

Delphiniums, larkspur and the fancy grasses, except for a slight change in colour, respond very well to this treatment. I myself prefer to handle them by this method rather than by air-drying. It renders them so much more supple and lifelike. Beech leaves are simply marvellous done this way. After about three weeks with the stems in the solution, the leaves become supple and satiny, and they change colour, becoming in some cases a curious, beautiful bronze-olive green, in others, a golden chestnut. The kind of colour depends on the time of year the leaves are picked and preserved, and also varies with the tree. After three to four weeks remove the branches, place in a well-ventilated cupboard, and protect them

from dust. It is now immaterial whether you use them in water or dry.

Should the plant stem or leaf branch not be taking up the glycerine and water, which can be seen in a slight withering of the leaves, quickly remove the branch, shorten the stem end and in addition peel away some of the bark. Meanwhile, heat the glycerine and water solution and replace the treated branches. They ought to then take up the glycerine, unless they were too withered. In that case it is best to start afresh with a new branch or stem of the material you wish to preserve.

Oak leaves, sweet chestnut, magnolia leaves, eucalyptus (the latter turn out a lovely mauve-grey in some species, smoky-blue in others) and many other deciduous and evergreens, lend themselves wonderfully well to this type of preservation. Do not be afraid to experiment.

The evergreen foliage of Azara microphylla is another lovely subject for this method. Bruise or crush the stems well, and place them in the glycerine and water mixture. After about three weeks to a month, the leaves will become a gorgeous mahogany colour, and the foliage will now last

for months on end, in or out of water. When preserved in this way, this is a wonderful shrub for Christmas decorating. Paint it with copper, gold or silver metal paint (the powdered kind you buy at the art shops for painting metal or wooden picture surrounds or mirror frames). You prepare the paint yourself, using the liquid sold with it. While the paint is still wet, shake the spray of leaves in a paper bag holding glitter in the same or contrasting colour. It is most effective if some of the mahogany-brown, sometimes almost black, colour of the foliage is left unpainted to give depth to the brightness of paint and glitter. So do refrain from completely covering the leaves with paint.

The unpainted portions may be touched with clear varnish and glitter. Some of the privets and laurustinus family also respond well to this treatment, and so does holly that you may wish to use for Christmas. However, the glycerine will make the holly go a deep brown in colour and lose its colourful edging. Nevertheless, if preserved in this way it can be painted gold or silver and used for Christmas decoration. It will sometimes last for as long as two Christmas seasons, as against the unpreserved holly which wilts after a week or perhaps longer in water (considerably less, out of water).

Pampas grasses preserved with glycerine remain silky and do not shred their fluff as they tend to do if air or water-dried. Bullrushes also respond well, although they may still pop open in very warm rooms. Figwort seeds are also most receptive to this treatment, becoming very flexible and a delight to use. A quick drink of glycerine of about twenty-four hours' duration will put a sheen on the buds of the pussy-willow, after which it can be placed in water over and over again during the long summer months and then dried for the winter. Clematis, commonly known as 'old man's beard', if picked when very young and only tight green spirals, responds very well indeed, its foliage turning a mahogany brown. However, take care to defoliate each piece quite considerably before treating, as too many leaves not only look unattractive but will also drink the glycerine at a most expensive rate.

As you pick and use your flowers, foliage and seed heads, and branches of various trees, try out various ways of preserving them. You will find that many will react favourably to one of the three methods described.

Flowers preserved in borax: In addition to the methods given above, flower heads can also be preserved in borax. As is usual with all preserving, to obtain the best results the flowers must be cut when young. They are then placed in a box which is lined with a good helping of borax (about 3 inches thick). Lay the flower heads, each separate from its neighbour, face down on the powder and then proceed to cover completely with more borax. Each flower must be entirely covered. Place in a hot cupboard. Feel for dryness after thirty-six hours in the case of very delicate light-textured materials, such as pansies, clematis, cosmos, daffodils and all narcissus, deutzia, violets, cornflower, Queen Anne's lace and curly young fronds of fern. These varieties are usually preserved in this time. Roses, and other heavier-textured flowers, should be ready in about one week — also gladioli, kniphofia, spirea, stock, carnations, marigolds and some lilies.

All flowers and materials preserved in this way retain their beauty of colouring, but they require careful watching to see they are not kept in the borax after they are dry. If left too long they will disintegrate. Also, when using these flower heads, one has to be very light-fingered because they are so fragile. Wire them with a light-grade wire and expect quite a few casualties. It is wise to be prepared and do a few extra.

Finding precious bits and pieces of living materials to be preserved for future flower arrangements makes walking in the woods or by the sea even more delightful every year. Bracken cinnamon and sensitive ferns and coarse growers,

preferring wet places, are most decorative. These can be dried by pressing between sheets of newspaper and laying them under the drawing-room carpet.

But be sure it is an area where they will not get walked on too much or they will disintegrate.

Seed pods like poppy, rose, iris, regale lily, nigella and broom dry marvellously. All berries can be preserved after drying by painting them over with artist's clear picture varnish (likewise ornamental gourds), the idea being to keep out the air which otherwise would cause them to wither. A Finn once told me that in his country they preserve berries successfully over a long period by coating them in pure paraffin, which can be bought at most chemists and arrives as a solid block of white substance remarkably like cooking fat. After melting it, remove it from the heat, and, just before it starts to congeal, quickly dip the berries in and out. I have tried this method, sometimes with great success. However, gauging just the right moment to immerse the berries so that they do not either cook or congeal is quite an art in itself!

Branches of magnolia, wisteria and cotinus, to name just a few, particularly those with unusual

An antique incense burner holds an early winter-into-spring arrangement of pussy willow, preserved glossy black azara foliage, preserved laurustinus leaves, and working towards the centre, golden elaeagnus leaves and lime-green cupressus. Against this rich colouring, the actaea, paper-white and cheerful narcissi hold their own most wonderfully

Bracken, freshly picked dried dock and fool's parsley maintain their natural association when combined with this container of attractive lichen-covered bark

shapes and graceful curves are excellent if cleaned and put away for winter and early spring use. They are especially useful for Japanese and silhouette arrangements. You should also make a point of searching for branches of dead ivy to be found in the woods. They have the most odd and fascinating twists and turns, and will inspire you to create many artistic flower pictures, with a piece or two of the ivy used in place of flowers or living branches. They may also be used as an **accessory. The arrangement on page 157 is held** in a well-pinholder, which is all but concealed by a couple of pointed briony leaves. The ivy branch is set with Plasticine directly upon the top slab of Delabole slate, which is the base. Together with the ivy, it provides the inspiration for this very

elegant simple line design, vibrant with its strong rhythm of repetition. As you can see, the branch establishes the main line and is followed in its graceful movement by the beech mast and pods of the horned poppy. Black-eyed, brilliantly coloured gaillardias form the focal point at the convergence of all stems, and lead the eye into the swing of the movement.

If a branch is very discoloured wash it in a weak solution of household bleach, and dry it in the open air. When it is quite dry you can, if necessary, peel or strip it with a sharp knife till you obtain a smooth whiteness. Pieces of drift-wood, found on the beach and at the river's edge, will benefit by the same treatment, although they may not require washing.

These particularly require the most careful scraping with a very short, very sharp knife or scalpel, which enables you to get into all the crooks and crevices. A somewhat heavy piece can be lightened in texture by intensive chiselling away at it, and this adds to the joy of the find and makes it truly your own creation. I have many such pieces which I treasure (one of them is shown in use on page 149, and another favourite on page 154).

Branches of eucalyptus, preserved in glycerine and water, become a delightful smoky-mauve colour. Dark brown magnolia leaves are used in conjunction with another piece of driftwood to form a background to just one perfect chrysanthemum and bud. They have been encouraged to curl and wave by being removed from the preserving solution from time to time, and gently massaged into the desired shapes. Such natural containers can be most wonderfully fashioned from materials found all around us. But first we must cultivate the seeing eye as I term it: that capacity to look beyond the object as it is and visualise what it can become and what original and delightful purposes can be found for it. For some further attractive examples of dried-and-living arrangements, see colour plates 30, page 115, and 36, 37, pages 143, 144.

I do hope I have said enough to fire your imagination, and to make visits to country and seashore doubly interesting. In the woods, an exceptionally rich source, you can spend delightful hours searching for amusing bits of bark, odd branches, roots the wood-cutters may have left behind, and various attractive fungi, all of which will help towards the fashioning of made-up containers. By discovering and preserving these materials, so gratuitously provided for our delight in summer, we may continue to enjoy their beauty and their new colourings over the long months of winter. From such simple ingredients we can create works of art throughout the year, to bring beauty into our homes at practically no cost beyond the expenditure of a little time and energy.

Index